Developing Leadership Excellence

A Practice Guide for the New Professional Supervisor

Developing Leadership Excellence

A Practice Guide for the New Professional Supervisor

Tracey Harris

A PRODUCTIVITY PRESS BOOK

First published 2018
by Routledge
2 Park Square, Milton Park, Abingdon, Oxon OX14 4RN

and by Routledge
711 Third Avenue, New York, NY 10017

Routledge is an imprint of the Taylor & Francis Group, an informa business

© 2018 Taylor & Francis

International Standard Book Number-13: 978-0-8153-4637-1 (hbk)

International Standard Book Number-13: 978-0-8153-4636-4 (pbk)

International Standard Book Number-13: 978-1-351-17056-7 (ebk)

Library of Congress Cataloging-in-Publication Data

Names: Harris, Tracey, author.
Title: Developing leadership excellence : a practice guide for the new professional supervisor /
Tracey Harris.
Description: New York, NY : Routledge, 2018. | Includes bibliographical references and index. |
Identifiers: LCCN 2018003942 (print) | LCCN 2018025336 (ebook) | ISBN 9781351170567 (ebook) |
ISBN 9780815346371 (hardback : alk. paper) | ISBN 9780815346364 (pbk. : alk. paper)
Subjects: LCSH: Supervision of employees. | Leadership.
Classification: LCC HF5549.12 (ebook) | LCC HF5549.12 .H37 2018 (print) | DDC 658.3/02--dc23
LC record available at https://lccn.loc.gov/2018003942

This book is dedicated to all the professionals I have ever had the pleasure of working with in supervision. To everyone across psychology, social work, counselling, allied health, the corporate and business sectors, human services, government and non-government sectors both in Australia and globally, thank you for your support and commitment to professional supervision. You are making the professional world a much better place.

Contents

Acknowledgements

This book could not have been written without the generosity and commitment of all the professionals who have participated in supervision over many years. Thank you to all the professionals I have worked with in supervision throughout my career. Thank to you my wonderful colleague Nicola Payne, who has been inspirational as a professional in supporting the writing of this book and for your formatting expertise. To my editorial support, Alexandria Gryder, thank you for your support in the development of this book. Thank you to my publisher Michael Sinocchi from Taylor & Francis Group for your wonderful support and belief in such a book. I have thoroughly enjoyed this journey because of you.

I would also like to thank a few professionals who have always been there for encouragement and support not only in writing this book but also in supporting me throughout my career. To Dr. Ronnie Egan from RMIT for your time and commitment in my PhD studies, and to Professor Peter Camilleri for always believing in me and being the drive to keep writing. Dr. Jennifer Smith, thank you for being an inspiration to me as an academic and professional. You were the reason I was able to achieve my dream to teach in academia. Dr. Maddy Slattery, you are one of the most wonderful and committed professionals I have ever met. Having you alongside me in the journey of my PhD studies has been inspirational. Thank you for your time and colleagueship. I would like to particularly acknowledge Dr. Ming-sum Tsui, who has tirelessly given his career to the pursuit of quality supervision and has made a marked impact on me as a professional. You are a very special person and professional that I am truly blessed to have as a mentor and colleague. There are so many more professionals and colleagues to mention. You are all in my mind as I write this, and I thank you for your wisdom, support and encouragement.

Foreword

Professional supervision is the most important professional relationship you can ever have. When rapport is developed well, the professional supervisor can be instrumental in supporting and developing you in your role. A skilled supervisor supports you to consciously reflect on your work, using key frameworks to evidence your daily work.

In this guide, Tracey has brought together a wealth of knowledge and information designed to support the new supervisor to develop supervisory excellence. The book addresses an important transition in the career of a helping professional, namely that from practitioner to supervisor, and also highlights the need for guidance for those undertaking that transition. The author makes a compelling case for formal supervision education and training and provides excellent material to support new supervisors in this area. The road map presented assists new supervisors to enhance their understanding of supervision and to develop their supervisor competence and capability. The chapters are practically focused and provide the reader with many practical tools and reflective exercises that are derived from the author's scholarship, experience as a trainer and extensive background as a professional supervisor. In short, this book is an important part of the new supervisor's framework and contains the valuable practice wisdom shared from an expert and experienced supervisor. It is full of gems that will assist the new supervisor to provide quality and excellent supervision. I encourage readers to engage with this book, undertake the reflective questions, use the exemplars and complete the questions and activities in this book, because they will help you grow and develop as a new supervisor towards supervisory excellence.

Dr. Kieran O'Donoghue, PhD
Associate Professor and Head of the School of Social Work
Massey University New Zealand

Preface

Professional supervision underpins the very essence of allied health, social work, psychology, and the business and human service arenas. It is the cornerstone of our work that enables professionals to debrief and strengthen every aspect of their role. When supervision is present, it assists a practitioner to refuel on a regular basis, cope with the many complexities that are present and use the supervisory conversation as a debriefing mechanism. Without it, rates of fatigue and burnout continue to increase throughout many professions (Tsui, 2005). In the UK, United States, Australia and other countries, many staff in professional or clinical roles have access to professional supervision; however, human resource, administration and operational support staff are often not afforded the same opportunities, despite it being important to maintain high performance in the workplace (Bogo & McKnight, 2006; Carroll, 2007b).

Professional supervision is crucial to make sound decisions on a daily basis, maintain good health and well-being in the workplace and ensure effective service outcomes are achieved for the clients and customers that our work focuses on. Supervision assists staff to reflect on what they are doing in their role, how they are doing it and why they approach things in the way they do. Professional supervision is one of the fundamental elements to maintaining professional standards, and it provides a quarantined time and space to stop on a regular basis to feel heard and valued without the noise and interruption of a busy workplace (Morrison & Wonnacott, 2010; Watkins & Milne, 2014).

This supervisor practice guide has been written with you as the new supervisor, coach or leader in mind. As a new supervisor, it is important that you are adequately supported as you start in your role, and having a book to guide you is one of the most effective ways to do this. This book has been written to support you as you navigate the many elements required to step into your new role. I hope this guide assists you to establish an effective supervision framework and process that will enable you to take on the supervisory role with confidence, enthusiasm and commitment.

Congratulations on your new role. Remember to ensure you receive effective and quality supervision yourself – you deserve it!

Introduction

Where It All Began

The most effective type of supervision is that which ensures you reflect on a regular basis and that assists you to produce better outcomes and results in your role. Supervision develops your skills and opens your mind to always learn new things. It refuels you for a few weeks until your next supervision meeting. It allows you to refocus and clarify things and at the same time, it allows you to have someone who is encouraging and values you as a professional.

A quick reference practice guide can be one of the most valuable books for a new supervisor as you commence your supervisory career. I recall when I provided supervision for the first time early in my career. I wanted to ensure that I did a good job. I also wanted to ensure that I met the needs of the professionals I was supervising; however, at times I was unsure of what I was meant to be doing. Whilst I was lucky enough to have been introduced to supervision by an experienced supervisor, it was still a daunting experience starting out in the role for the first time. I had not attended training prior to becoming a supervisor as good training was difficult to find.

When we begin our career as a supervisor, we often first use what I refer to when facilitating training as the 'wing it' model. This means that we provide supervision predominantly based on our own experiences of supervision or what others have told us about their experiences in supervision. Over time, as we hone and shape our skills, gain more knowledge through training and understand relevant supervision skills we need to have, we grow to develop our own framework and process in the role. Over the years, I have developed and shaped specific technical skills, knowledge and competences, attended many different training programs and ensured that I have had effective supervision myself. As a result, I have come to truly understand the complexity in which quality professional and line management supervision takes place. I also understand the role that supervision plays in a range of practice and organisational contexts, and I know it takes time to practice the skills that supervisors need to have to do the role well (Gonsalvez et al., 2017; Kracen, 2015).

When I reflect on my career, I see that I was lucky enough to receive quality supervision from my first supervisor. I work with hundreds of supervisors and supervisees across the world and enjoy hearing about their experiences in supervision. Sadly, I hear many stories of supervision not being a positive or useful experience, and often the reasons are that the supervisor has not attended training or has not had quality supervision themselves. My first supervisor was competent and I learned a lot about the skills and knowledge required to provide effective supervision. I have often thought about what was unique about that supervisor and if she was providing supervision like many others do. I have come to the conclusion that my supervisor at the time was somewhat exceptional because of the way she provided supervision, the skills and knowledge she had and her awareness of how to engage me in the reflective process. No matter what we were discussing or focusing on, her supervisory style was positive and she challenged me to be my best as a professional. This provided me with a solid foundation that supported me when I started in a supervisory role. Since that time, I have grown and developed as a supervisor, and I am always reading and learning different aspects of being a supervisor and supervision itself.

Having said that, I have also had some not-so-great experiences of professional supervision. This has equally provided me with the opportunity to compare and understand the differences between good, high-quality and inadequate supervision. All experiences, good and not so good, are useful and inform our own supervisory practice. At the same time, I would be naïve to say that everyone I have supervised has enjoyed my style or approach. However, it is important to be committed to every person you supervise and use the range of skills and competencies required to provide effective supervision (Jacobsen & Tanggaard, 2009).

I would have found it helpful to have a new supervisor practice guide when I was starting as a brand-new supervisor – a quick reference guide to validate I was on the right track. It would have really assisted me to build my confidence initially, so I hope this is useful for you. This guide is designed for you as a new professional and/or line management supervisor. You may work in corporate services or manage your own business. You may be working in mental health, human resources, allied health, physiotherapy, social work or psychology. You may be a supervisor of an operational team or in human services. You may be supervising a professional or clinical team, or your leadership role may be in private practice. You may also be starting to supervise students. Wherever you may be working, this guide is for you. I hope you find this guide useful and cannot put it down until the end!

How to Use This Book

This book consists of seven chapters. It is best read in sequence as it has been written as a guide that you can follow from start to finish. At the end of each chapter, there are reflective questions for you to consider that mirror each step in the supervisory process.

Documenting your reflections along the way will support you to

- Capture what you are thinking at the time when you read the chapter
- Take the time and space to express what you are thinking and feeling at the time of writing
- Reflect more deeply on your thinking and increase the skill of reflection
- Develop a plan to support you in your new role
- Maintain notes and records of your thinking at the time of writing
- Reflect: reflection is brain friendly as it takes us away from task and process and helps us dig beneath the surface of our thinking

The questions at the end of each chapter also have another purpose! They are designed for you to reflect and also to use with the staff you supervise. All the information in this book provides you with practical information and resources that are useful for both you and the professionals you supervise. The tools included in this guide can be used as discussion points in supervision conversations and can support you to set up your supervision framework.

This guide is not designed to be a comprehensive set of resources and tools or a theoretical book. It is a practical book to get you started on the right track.

With this in mind, it is important to

- Continue to engage in further reading on supervision
- Continue to learn and understand additional aspects of supervision
- Over time, ensure that you evaluate the effectiveness of the supervision you provide to keep learning and growing
- Where possible, attend reputable training on supervision prior to commencing in your new role
- Reflect on your supervisory practice with your supervisor on a regularbasis

The chapters in the book include useful information about

- Understanding different contexts of the supervisory environment
- Setting up the first supervisory meeting
- How to conduct subsequent meetings
- Understanding what to record in supervision meetings
- Understanding how to ensure that every supervision meeting is effective
- Understanding the difference between line management and professional supervision
- Evaluating supervision to ensure it remains effective

The quotes below are others' ideas on what supervision is:

At its simplest, supervision is a forum where supervisees review and reflect on their work in order to do it better. In a relationship of trust and transparency, supervisees talk about their work through a reflective process. (Carroll, 2007b, p. 36)

Supervision is a formal process of professional support, central to the role of learning. Supervision in varying forms has been shown to be effective in increasing job satisfaction, reducing stress and burnout and improving quality outcomes. (Wallbank & Hatton, 2011, p. 31)

Author

Tracey Harris is the executive director of Amovita International and is a leading speaker on developing high performance in the workplace. Tracey has worked in the human services and corporate sectors specialising in organisational and business excellence, leadership and performance for over 25 years.

Throughout her career, Tracey has worked in various leadership roles including being a senior ministerial advisor where her portfolio responsibilities included community and public housing reform as well homelessness policy specialising in indigenous affairs. She has worked for State and Federal Members of Parliament focusing on family and domestic violence and education policy reform. Her clinical practice experience spanned twelve years where she worked in relationship counselling, men's perpetrator programs, long-term unemployment, clinical mental health and children and family programs. Tracey also provided lectureship at the Australian Catholic University in Brisbane, Australia teaching in the areas of public and social policy, clinical social work practice, field education and organisational practice.

Tracey leads the Strategy and Executive Consulting Division within Amovita and she works with leaders, managers and business owners both in Australia and internationally to support high performance in the workplace. She has developed an integrated model of supervision and coaching and is currently a PhD candidate with Griffith University in Brisbane focused on developing a supervision capability framework for supervisors and leaders in the workplace.

Understanding the Role of Supervision

> Whilst it is important to use your own knowledge, skills and experience in supervision, it is equally important to understand the range of skills your supervisor has, so these may add value to your own.

Congratulations, you are about to embark on one of the most important professional roles you will have in your career. Now that you are about to become a professional or line management supervisor, it is useful to reflect on what has brought you to this point; what professional experiences you have had that have led here and why you would like to take on this role. You may already be in a leadership role and have found yourself moving into a supervisory role because it is an organisational requirement. You may have applied for a new role as a supervisor, or you may have your own business or private practice and now need to supervise others. Keep these thoughts in mind as you read this book. Over time it will be interesting for you to review your thoughts, see if you think differently and observe how you grow and develop in the role.

Being a professional or line management supervisor in any workplace is a role that brings with it many rewards and some challenges. Whilst there are many rewards, there will be times where you wonder why you took on the role. Why? It is a role that requires a specific set of skills and knowledge to do the job well, so this takes time to develop. It can often feel as though you don't really have the time to provide supervision given all the other things that are on your plate, but overall it is a wonderful role where you have the opportunity to support your staff to develop and grow in their roles, ensure they feel valued and supported as well as provide them with insight and skills to maintain their role to a high standard.

Your new role is a serious commitment for both you and your supervisee(s) given what supervision is intended to provide. Prior to becoming a supervisor, it is worth talking to another trusted professional supervisor about how they have set up their own supervisory framework, to understand what the highs and lows of the role have been and discuss any tips they can impart to make the role easier. It is always useful to know some of the shortcuts and pitfalls that others have experienced so that you don't have to reinvent the wheel. It is also important to have a mentor or coach as you commence in the role to guide and support you, as it will help you develop confidence in your supervisory role from the start. One word of caution, though – try to only listen to the constructive and positive things from others. You certainly don't want to be put off from the start with too many negative experiences or feedback that others may have. This will also ensure that you will do the same for others in the future (O'Donoghue, 2015).

Over time, your new role will influence many aspects of the supervisees' role. It will change their thinking about particular approaches and aspects of their work, stretch their values and beliefs, enhance their skills and knowledge as well as support their professional well-being. There will be many times where you will impact significantly a supervisee's professional career. As professional and line management supervisors, we may think we are just doing our job on a daily basis; however, being a supervisor is far more than that. It is a professional role that requires specific skills, knowledge and capabilities. In many workplaces, the supervisor role requires a separate position description demonstrating the important role it plays.

Let's think back to when you were at school, played a sport, were in a club or had a hobby. There is usually at least one teacher or coach who you may remember the most, someone who knew what to say at the right moment, encouraged you and were there to debrief and talk about things during the tough times. Someone who challenged you and provided feedback to practice a certain skill and think about what you were doing from a particular aspect.

I can remember my first hockey coach, Mrs Cowgill. She coached me from grade one when I was just six years old right through to the end of high school. She was always encouraging us, even when she was firm in her instruction and direction. Mrs Cowgill continued to coach us lovingly when we lost a game. I saw her recently at a restaurant and again she beamed when we greeted each other after not seeing each other for many years.

I thanked her for her wisdom and for being such an important part of my life from childhood. Her legacy has carried me through my professional years as the skills and knowledge she gave me and the team have been immeasurable.

Supervision is similar. Over time it can leave a lasting impression on us. Our supervisors are part of our professional journey and are part of our story – just like Mrs Cowgill. Supervision is therefore not just a conversation. It is a professional relationship that journeys with us in our professional role through time. Just like a hockey coach, the supervisor knows how to guide and develop the supervisee, knows how to get the best out of the supervisee, uses the right language to positively challenge and also be there through the tough times. It is a complex and multilayered approach that is dynamic and relational. It is a professional process that can transform the practice and conduct of any employee (Carroll, 2010).

Let's see how supervision has made a difference to a supervisee:

> I have received professional supervision for much of my professional life. I have been qualified in my profession for 15 years and have had internal supervision as a requirement of my role. I have also had external supervision throughout my career. It's really only been in the last year with my current supervisor that I have come to understand what this 'thing' called supervision is all about. I feel like I have awakened for the first time in my career and wonder what I have been doing with my own supervisees for all this time. (Supervisee Sam)

Different Types of Supervision

It is important to have a clear understanding of what supervision is and the different types of supervision that you may provide. You will hear different terms being used to define supervision, such as the following:

- Professional supervision
- Clinical supervision
- Practice supervision
- Interprofessional supervision
- Disciplinary or interdisciplinary specific supervision
- Line supervision

- Operational supervision
- Administrative supervision
- Professional conversations
- Coaching
- Mentoring
- Management supervision
- Group supervision
- Peer or collegial supervision
- Adhoc supervision
- Formal supervision
- Informal supervision

When you commence supervision with a new supervisee, if you are an internal supervisor (within the organisation) or an external supervisor (from outside of the organisation), it is important to understand what type of supervision you are providing and to be clear with the supervisee about the type of supervision they will be receiving. This supports you to set up the appropriate framework and documents relevant to the supervisee's work and know the focus of discussions. For example, if you are providing line management or operational supervision, conversations will predominantly focus on the requirements of the role as detailed in their position description.

If you are providing clinical or professional supervision, discussions will revolve around the supervisee's practice and client work. Ensure the supervisee understands your role as this sets the boundaries of how supervision is provided, the process that you will engage, how supervision discussions will be documented and the type of supervision they will be provided (Beddoe & Davys, 2010; Carroll, 2007b; O'Donoghue, 2015; Watkins & Milne, 2014).

Figure 1.1 provides a brief description of the different types of supervision.

Now that we have explored the different types of supervision that you may provide, let's think about someone you have known who has inspired you throughout your life.

Think about a teacher, sports coach or mentor you had growing up who you felt inspired by, who supported you and was interested in you.

How long did you know them for?

_____

_____

_____

Clinical

Supervision is provided in a clinical setting i.e. hospital or health setting. Supervision discussions include specific clinical discussion about patients' diagnosis etc. and looks at clinical interventions. Clinical supervision has a heavy emphasis on the practices of the supervisee and their clinical approach, theories and interventions.

Professional

Professional supervision is provided in a clinical or non-clinical setting. It explores clinical interventions and outcomes or non-clinical approaches that the supervisee is using with clients. Professional supervision discussion explores the professional's role, organisational requirements, support for the supervisee and focuses on developmental aspects of the supervisee, professional identity and client cases.

Discipline specific

Supervision is provided by a professional that is from the same profession or discipline as the supervisee (for example a physiotherapist supervising a physiotherapist, social worker supervising a social worker etc.).

Transdiscipline

Supervision is provided by a supervisor who is supervising staff across a number of roles, practice areas or organisations. The supervisor is skilled in being able to provide supervision to staff in various organisational contexts.

Peer

Supervision is conducted by peers or colleagues in the same organisation, team or from across different organisations with a similar practice focus. Supervisees are usually on the same organisational level.

Informal

Supervision is provided adhoc or on an irregular basis. Supervisory discussion may be held as a casual discussion and may be referred to as a 'corridor discussion' or conversations on the run throughout the week. Minutes may or may not be recorded.

Operational

Supervision is provided by the supervisees line or operational manager within the organisation and focuses on the administrative elements of the supervisees role. Supervision is more concerned with meeting deadlines and detail of the supervisees position description. This supervision is often also referred to as operational or administrative supervision.

Formal

This is supervision that has a formal context to it. It has a clear structure and framework. The supervisor uses a range of relevant documents that form part of the professional process. Supervision is provided on a regular basis and is frequently evaluated. A supervision model is ideally used to guide the discussion and evaluate the effectiveness of supervision. Minutes are taken from each meeting and follow a formal process. Supervision discussions focuses on four areas including the professional practice context, organisational requirements, support of the supervisee and has an educational component as well.

Group

Supervision is provided by a supervisor with a group or professionals in the same organisation or role area. Group size is limited to 6 or 7 supervisees and the facilitator may be changed each group supervision meeting or is maintained by the same person i.e. supervisor or group member. Members of the group decide if the supervision provided is for a closed or open group. An open group sees members come in and out of the group and a closed group has the same membership for a period of time with no new members entering the group on a regular basis.

Figure 1.1 Types of Supervision.

What do you remember the most about them?

_____

_____

_____

How did they inspire, support or positively challenge you?

_____

_____

_____

What skills and knowledge did they have?

What do you remember about their language, how they interacted with you and supported you?

Fantastic! Some of the things that you have reflected on will help you to consider what type of supervisor you want to be. Take the best from those who have inspired you. Be the leader of others that you want to be remembered for. Consider how you want to inspire those professionals who you supervise and how you want to build and maintain the professional relationship. All of these things are crucial in being an effective professional and/or line management supervisor.

Now that you have reflected on someone who you admire or who has inspired you, let's think about what you already know about supervision. Don't worry too much if you are not sure about what supervision is at this point; just explore the following questions with curiosity. As you reflect, it is useful to write down your responses. After you have attended training or if you have already attended supervision training, come back to these questions and review to see if you would change your earlier responses.

1. This is what I know about professional and line management supervision:

---

2. My definition of supervision is:

---

3. The purpose of supervision is:

---

4. Supervision needs to achieve the following outcomes:

_____

_____

_____

5. This is what I think the benefits are from providing or receiving supervision:

_____

_____

_____

6. The impact of not receiving supervision can be:

_____

_____

_____

7. I believe that poor or inadequate supervision looks like:

_____

_____

_____

8. I think supervision is not about:

_____

_____

_____

9. Supervisors need to have the following skills, knowledge and attributes to remain effective in the role:

_____

_____

_____

Defining Supervision

Professional Supervision

A lot has been written about supervision, and if you read or do some research on supervision, there are many and varied definitions and explanations. Professional and line management supervision is integral to providing quality service and practice outcomes for the clients and staff who we work with.

Quality supervision is undertaken by a professional who is appropriately trained and qualified to provide supervision (Carroll, 2010). It is a professional conversation held on a regular basis between a supervisor and supervisee to engage in a process of reflection, enable support and guidance to the supervisee in their role and maintain their high performance over time. Supervision is also a professional discussion that has intention, meaning and purpose. It is focused on key aspects of the supervisee's role and is outcome based.

Discussions are strengths-based using language that develops and grows the professional over time. Supervision is an interactive process based on coaching and mentoring principles that assists to maintain the supervisee's skills whilst achieving both professional and practice outcomes. It upholds professional identity as the key pillar of one's self in practice. Professional supervision facilitates a process of maintaining key skills in a supportive professional relationship (Baldwin, 2004; Egan, 2012; Egan, Maidment, & Connolly, 2016; Tsui, 2005).

Line Management or Managerial Supervision

Line management supervision is usually undertaken by the supervisee's manager ensuring that the supervisee fulfils the requirements of their role as prescribed by their position description. It is more concerned about what the organisation needs the employee to do in the role. It predominantly focuses discussion on the tasks and processes of the role rather than the practice, development or support of the individual. Line management supervision is often also referred to as administrative, managerial or operational supervision.

If supervisors only use this type of supervision, over time supervisees can feel that supervision is a little stale and is only focused on organisational needs rather than the supervisees themselves. Given the nature of the role, it is important that the supervisor bring a balance to the discussion for the supervisee to feel valued and supported rather than just having discussions about what the organisational needs are (Falender & Shafranske, 2012; O'Donoghue, 2015; Watkins & Milne, 2014).

Given what we have explored so far, Table 1.1 provides an overview of what supervision is and the things you may discuss in supervision meetings. The table overviews the four key areas of focus in supervision discussions. The first area is about the professional and how they engage and practice in their role. The second area of the supervision discussion looks at what organisational requirements may be discussed in the role. The third

Table 1.1 Focus of Supervision Discussions

Professional/Practice	*Organisational/Administrative*
The how, what and why of the supervisees' work. Supervision focuses on reflection in the role and explores ethics and ethical dilemmas. Understanding appropriate professional approaches in the supervisees' work. Supports the focus of the supervisees' work through their professional framework and decision-making processes. Developing and maintaining a professional identity in the role.	Discussion focuses on the tasks and processes in the role, policies and procedures, budgets, projects, planning, all administrative aspects to the role. Resource allocation, compliance, accreditation, continuous improvement, reporting, monthly reporting, client or customer satisfaction, statistics, documentation, case note processes, evaluation processes, human resources, performance in the role, annual review process.
Educative/Professional Development	*Support/Person*
Maintaining professional excellence. Growth and development. Conference presentations, transfer of learning from any training into the role. Training needs, maintenance of competencies and skills, research, use of evidence base.	Health and well-being. team dynamics, self-care, work and life balance, beliefs and values, workplace relationships, job and role satisfaction, personal responsibility and professional accountability, refuelling, debriefing, being supported, encouraged, appreciated and supported in the role.

area is about the person and support of them in their role, and the final area is about the development of the supervisee in their role (Kadushin & Harkness, 2014).

Now might be a good time to go back to see how you defined supervision in the previous questions. Was it close to the definitions you have just read?

Now that you have reflected on what you think supervision is and considered the different types of supervision, here are some questions for you to think about in terms of the supervision you will be providing to others. The following questions are also useful to explore with your own supervisor. They are also useful questions to ask your supervisees so you can gain their understanding and reflections on what they believe supervision is.

Questions to Reflect on as a New Supervisor

The supervision I am going to provide will be effective because of:

_____

_____

_____

I know that I receive quality supervision myself when:

_____

_____

_____

I am going to evaluate the effectiveness of the supervision I provide by:

_____

_____

_____

The model of supervision I am going to use is:

_____

_____

_____

The skills and knowledge I already have as a supervisor include:

_____

_____

_____

I am interested in being a supervisor because:

_____

_____

_____

The following questions are also important to explore with your supervisee early on in the supervisory relationship.

What do you think supervision is?

_____

_____

Is there anything that you would like to know about me as a supervisor?

_____

_____

_____

What things would you like me to know about you?

_____

_____

_____

What is the most effective way to seek feedback from you about how
supervision is going?

_____

_____

_____

What approach would you like me to use in our conversations?

_____

_____

_____

Now that you have started to think more deeply about your new role,
there are just a few more things to consider. Before you commence in the
role, start to develop a list of things to do so that you know you are ready
to go. First, consider the need to attend reputable quality training. Ask
your professional circles about what supervision training others have been
to, what the training includes and the cost per day. The training program
needs to have both a theoretical and practice component and provide
you with the pathway to transfer your learning back into the role almost
immediately.

Quality training has information, materials, articles, tools, resources and
frameworks that can be transferred directly back to your supervisory role.
Training materials need to include the latest evidence on supervision. If you
do not have the opportunity to use the information from the training, it
will start to disappear within a month after the training. We will talk more
about training in Chapter 3 (Carroll, 2010; Falender & Shafranske, 2012; Terry,
Gonsalvez, & Deane, 2017; Tsui & Cheung, 2004; Wolsfeld & Hay-Yahia, 2010).

Second, understand what process of supervision you are going to adopt.
This includes the documents you may need to develop and implement, if
you need to do any monthly reporting for your own manager or supervisor,
how minutes will be documented and stored and what will happen to the
supervisee's file if the supervisee moves to another supervisor or leaves their
role. Also consider what, if any, supervision model you will use to guide discussions and what the evaluation process will be to ensure that your supervision is effective.

Will you need to consider any cultural practices in supervision, and how might you do this if you have staff from a diverse range of cultures or backgrounds? All of these things will be covered in this guide; however, at this stage as you are reading, just consider the things that will be necessary. Finally, start to prepare yourself for the role. Be confident in what you already know, what experiences you may have had in supervision, and be open with supervisees about the fact that you are new to the role and learning alongside them. Most staff will be giving and forgiving as you have your learner's plates on in the role. We all have to start somewhere, and if you have been lucky enough to have quality supervision yourself, you will have some idea of how to start the process and, if not, this guide will be helpful as you get underway.

Appropriate Insurance

Many supervisors working in organisations and in private practice do not have adequate insurance. Insurance can be expensive, so it is good to shop around for it to be cost effective, particularly if you are in private practice or your own business. If you are going to be a supervisor in an organisation, they will most likely have their own professional indemnity and public liability insurance; therefore, you will not have to take out additional insurance. If you have a qualification in counselling, social work, psychology, community services or physiotherapy you may already be a member of your professional association and already have professional indemnity insurance.

Being a member of a professional association is important, not only for the opportunity to feed into relevant reviews, participate in committee forums and receive valuable information but also because you most probably will be covered with an appropriate level of professional indemnity and public liability insurance (AASW, 2014; AHPRA, 2017, NASW, 2013). Consider what level and type of insurance you think you may need if required and seek a number of quotes outlining the type of supervisory work you will be engaged in. Costs can be dependent on the services you provide, particularly if you are in a private practice or business, so it is useful to check what the policy covers. It is also worth checking with your professional association about the coverage you may have as part of your membership and what services are included in the policy to ensure you have adequate coverage.

Table 1.2   My Initial Checklist

√	*Supervisor Checklist*
	Identified appropriate supervision training
	Attended supervision training
	Thought about someone who has inspired me
	Documented the skills I have to be a supervisor
	Checked if I need insurance
	Understand the different types of supervision
	Engaged in my own quality supervision
	Talked to others about how they set up supervision
	Completed the reflective questions in this chapter

A search of insurances companies will provide you with a range of options, and then you can check which one suits you best. If you are a manager or supervisor in an organisation or business, you may not need any additional insurance coverage, so check with your direct line manager. Table 1.2 is a simple checklist of the things that may be required as you start in the role of a professional supervisor.

As we finish our first chapter about understanding the role of supervision, we have defined what supervision is and provided some reflective questions for you to consider as you commence in the role. You have thought about someone who has inspired you and documented what you remember most about them. As you go read through the chapter summary, review the great questions for you to consider as you start the role.

Chapter 1 Summary

Supervision is an important part of any employee's role. It provides the necessary support to provide quality outcomes in the role and a professional conversation that supports staff to reflect on what they do. Remember to attend training prior to commencing in the role if you can and check in with other supervisors who you know to understand the pitfalls of commencing in the role so you don't have to reinvent the process.

Your key points in understanding the role of supervision.
1.
2.
3.
4.
5.

Chapter 2

Line Management and Professional Supervision

The role of a line manager and professional supervisor is a delicate balancing act and must keep the professional relationship at the core of each discussion.

You will find a lot of information about the differences between line management and professional supervision. We covered the differences between line management and professional supervision in Chapter 1, and you will now have a clear idea of what type of supervision you will be providing. It is important to know something about both approaches, particularly if you find yourself in the role as a line manager and also professional supervisor.

Let's first explore the different ways that line management and professional supervision can be provided.

Think about your own experiences with a manager that you have had and what types of conversations have taken place. Your manager may have had discussions with you that were focused only on the role, whilst another manager may focus on aspects of the role but also discussed your professional development in the role. Before we explore the different ways that line management and professional supervision can be provided, think about the following questions.

My Experiences of Line Management Discussions

What types of things does your manager usually discuss with you?

_____

_____

_____

How do these conversations support you in your role?

_____

_____

_____

How do these conversations consider how to continue to grow
and develop you in the role?

_____

_____

_____

How do line management discussion meetings reflect on the professional
aspects of the role, your professional identity, how you engage decision-
making practices?

_____

_____

_____

Would you consider these meetings or conversations as supervision?

_____

_____

_____

Now that you have considered how your line management supervision
meetings are conducted, you may be receiving line management supervision
that focuses only on the organisational requirements of the role or a mix of
line management and professional supervision, where the manager balances
the discussion by exploring how you are doing in the role, exploring the
professional approaches you undertake in your role and how to continually
grow and develop you in the role.

Some supervisees have two separate supervisors where one provides
the line management supervision and another provides professional supervision. There are many professionals who have their line manager supervisor who is also their professional supervisor, therefore acting in a dual

supervisory role. Others may have their line manager from within the organisation and the professional supervision may be provided by another professional external to the organisation, often referred to as an external professional supervisor. Supervisors who are external to the organisation predominantly focus on the professional and educational aspects of the role.

Whilst there are benefits to having the same supervisor both as a line manager and professional supervisor – because the supervisor can then focus on all aspects of the supervisee – many professionals are moving to have their internal line manager/supervisor focus on the requirements of the role and a different supervisor either internal or external to the organisation to provide professional supervision.

Line Manager vs Professional Supervisor

As outlined in Figure 2.1, the line management supervisor is responsible for the day-to-day activities and performance of the supervisee to ensure operational, organisational and strategic goals are met. Line managers have the administrative responsibility to ensure adherence to structural processes, compliance with policy and organisational requirements and to monitor work practice (Falender & Shafranske, 2007, 2009). The role of the professional supervisor is not so much to deal with the performance of the supervisees in their role or respond to various management issues. This is the role of the line manager. Where the supervisor is both a line manager and professional supervisor, it is important to have a proper process in which any underperformance or performance management issues can be discussed, for example, in line management supervision discussions (Falender & Shafranske, 2008, 2012; Farmer, 2009).

The professional supervisor's role is to provide the supervisee with the space and opportunity to explore and maintain quality client outcomes through reflection on the practice components of their role. This role supports the supervisee to develop, enhance and maintain professional practice skills and knowledge, with a view to high performance outcomes. Professional supervision is a collaborative and positive process, a formal arrangement with an appropriately trained and experienced professional that facilitates quality client outcomes (Gillet et al., 2013; Shaw, 2004).

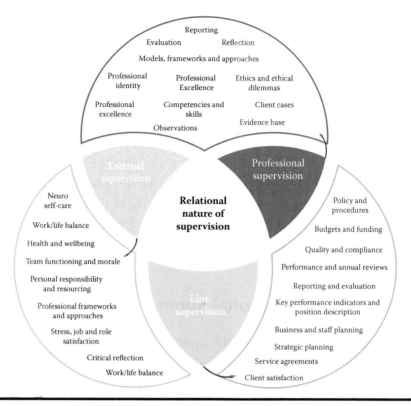

Figure 2.1 Relational nature of professional supervision.

If you are an external supervisor, it is important to get to know your supervisee's internal line manager where possible and form a three-way co-supervisory partnership in the supervisory process. Where this is possible, there is the opportunity to really support the supervisee and achieve the following:

■ Undertake a three-way evaluation of the effectiveness of supervision on an annual basis.
■ The external supervisor can provide valuable input to the supervisee's annual review from the external supervisory process.
■ The external supervisor can be a useful referee if the supervisee changes roles or jobs.
■ Themed feedback can be provided to the line manager about what is being achieved in supervision (remembering confidentiality principles and discussing level of feedback with the supervisee).

Some internal supervisors do not feel the need to get to know the external professional supervisor, but where you have the opportunity it can be useful to do a 'meet and greet'. If you are an external supervisor, there are a number of key questions you could ask the internal supervisor that demonstrate your willingness to work together in the supervisory alliance.

You could meet at times throughout the year to have a conversation about how supervision is progressing. At no time is confidentiality to be compromised, so it is important to have tools and frameworks to only discuss themes of the supervision discussion without disclosing any content and information about your detailed discussions.

Questions may include the following:

■ What might be the key things you could see us working on in supervision over the coming twelve months?
■ What reporting processes would you like to see in place?
■ How do you think we can work together to support the supervisee in our respective roles?
■ Do you think it would be useful to regularly discuss how things are going and, if so, how often?
■ Are there any things coming up in the organisation that may be useful for me to consider in our supervision meetings?
■ How can I be a support to you as the line manager with the focus of external supervision?

Reporting Requirements

If you are an external supervisor, many organisations require some form of report about how many meetings have taken place during the year, dates meetings have been held and what key areas have been a focus. This is particularly important if they are paying for the supervisee to engage in external supervision. Consider what is relevant and appropriate to include in a report if you are required to provide one, and remember that the detail of supervision is confidential, so provide an overview of supervision, thinking about what is confidential and what you can share. Having a range of supervision and professional tools is desirable as you can then refer to these in a report without compromising the integrity and confidentiality of professional supervision. Some organisations also require you to sign a formal contract when you commence supervision with staff, and it is important to reflect and consider the detail prior to signing the final copy.

If you are an internal supervisor, writing a report on an annual basis may also be useful. In many organisations, professional supervision is not afforded the time and value it requires to gain maximum benefit. Taking the opportunity to report on your commitment and process of supervision may provide the organisation with the impetus to see supervision as a valued activity. Many organisations also report on supervision in their monthly report to a board of management or senior management group, so being clear on what you are reporting on is crucial (Falender & Shafranske, 2012).

Balancing the Relationship as a Line Manager and Professional Supervisor

It is important to consider how to balance the relationship between line supervisor and professional supervisor for the reasons outlined above. When you commence supervision with a supervisee, discuss the challenges and boundaries that may be present in such a relationship and how you both might manage this. Because there is a dual role, you may find the supervisee holds back a little over time because you are in a position of authority, and this automatically sets up a power imbalance in the supervisor/supervisee relationship. It is important to have a clear approach to managing performance discussions if necessary, especially if the supervisee finds it difficult to provide feedback or have a conversation with you as the supervisor when things are not going well. Consider how you can protect the professional supervision relationship during those times.

Discussing these issues and challenges in the first meeting will assist to take some pressure off the dual relationship. Document what you discuss with clear strategies to use during any challenging times. Have a clear framework for communication around how you might put the professional supervision process on hold to discuss line manager issues, and how you might preserve this valuable process, so you can return to the professional supervisory relationship once you have moved through the challenges or issues. Some supervisors put the professional supervision on hold and engage a different process, so the professional supervision process is maintained as a positive and engaging process for both parties (Karpenko & Gidycz, 2012).

Chapter 2 Summary

Think about the differences between line and professional supervision. Consider what role you will have, that is, internal or external, line manager vs professional supervisor. If you are an external supervisor, endeavour to meet with the internal supervisor where appropriate in the spirit of a partnership approach. If you are in a dual role of line manager and professional supervisor, outline the two roles with the supervisee early on in the professional relationship. Consider what reporting requirements there may be about supervision on an annual basis, and maintain confidentiality and integrity of the discussions in supervision that take place.

Key things to consider in Chapter 2 about the difference between line and professional supervision.

1.
2.
3.
4.
5.

Chapter 3

Quality Supervision Training

> Optimal performance comes through great leadership. Great leadership is about developing others through effective conversations and being the right coach.

Becoming an experienced supervisor is a developmental journey. It takes time, ongoing development and an understanding of what existing skills and knowledge you already have as a professional. There are various things that contribute to the development of supervisors, and training is one of them. Many supervisors have never attended training and often do not engage in ongoing professional development to support their supervisory practice. Prior to becoming a professional supervisor, try to attend quality training. Engaging in training provides you with a range of resources and tools that will assist you to understand the skills necessary to provide supervision, how to establish the supervision process and to explore relevant supervision models to use in discussions (Blair & Peake, 1995; Kadushin & Harkness, 2014; Watkins & Milne, 2014).

Before we explore training, let's consider what other things are important for your ongoing development in between attending training and then beyond training. Even though you may be a new supervisor, you already have a broad range of emerging skills and abilities that you bring to the role. For example, you will have many transferable or portable skills and knowledge that you have gained from other roles and life experiences that will come with you into the supervisory role. You will have a range of abilities and skills that you gained at different ages and stages of your life, from your family upbringing and other environments, that all play an important part in where you are now.

What transferable skills do you think you will bring with you from your experiences into your supervisory role?

1.
2.
3.
4.
5.
6.
7.
8.
9.
10.

Other transferable skills may include how you like to communicate; the things that motivate you; what your key values and beliefs are; how organised you like to be; how you develop professional relationships; and how you like to learn, set goals and relate to others. Transferable skills (see Figure 3.1) are drawn from many aspects of your personality, attributes and thinking preferences and are used as you move from one role to another, through the different stages of your career and from organisation to organisation.

Training

Now that we have considered what transferable skills you will have to take into the supervisory role, let's think about what training may be useful to enhance your existing skills and knowledge. There are some great training programs available in professional supervision. Different professional associations advertise supervision training through their annual training calendars, so if you have membership in an association, check if they have an annual training calendar. It can also be useful to ask some of your colleagues to recommend training that they may know of or have attended. Your own supervisor or your organisation may also know of great supervision training.

When you have identified training that is of interest to you, it is worth calling the training organisation to speak with the facilitator or organiser to discuss what is included in the program or workshop, what level the training is pitched at and if it is the right one for you. It is not great when you attend training only to find that the material is not at the level of what you need

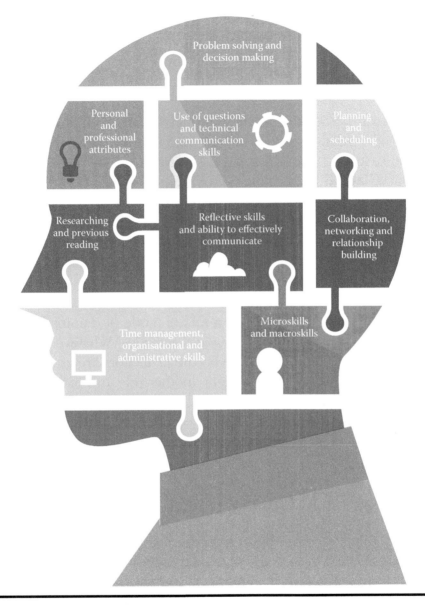

Figure 3.1 Transferable skills.

or where you have taken valuable time out of your work schedule to attend training that is not interesting or informative. It is great to attend training that validates your skills and knowledge; however, for you to use what is presented in training, it needs to have an element of new information contained in the program.

Quality training may cost a little more per day, but it is a worthwhile investment in the long term. It is also important to review the training flyer to ensure the topic areas listed can assist you to develop relevant supervisory skills you need in your new role. Remember, good training builds confidence, validates what you may already know and provides you with new information and skills (Bernard & Goodyear, 1992; Egan, 2012; Gonsalvez & Milne, 2010).

Also consider the duration of the training you are attending. Introductory or foundational training is often one day, and intermediate and advanced training can be two, three or five days. The training may be offered in shorter periods over a longer time period, that is, six to twelve months on a monthly basis, or can be delivered in two to three hour blocks of time each week or month for a period of time. This type of training is more conducive to effective learning, is far more brain friendly and allows you to learn and then embed new skills into your supervisory role. It also enhances existing skills and allows you time to test out in supervision what you have learned and then take these learnings back into the next training session.

Other training providers will offer a mixed mode of training that includes online, face-to-face and offline reading and activities. Whatever you decide is right for you, it is useful to know who the facilitators are and if they just provide training in supervision or are in another role and provide training in addition to their role. It is also important to understand if they receive professional supervision themselves. Having experienced and skilled facilitators makes the difference between good and excellent training (Proctor, 2000).

What to Look for in Quality Training

When considering attending supervision training, think about some of the following questions to ensure you choose training that is right for you.

- What topics do you think are useful for you as a new supervisor?
- What information are you looking for?
- What skills do you need to practice effective supervision?
- Do you want to go to training that focuses on only a couple of topics or is broader in its coverage of topic areas?
- What can the training offer you?
- How long do you want to attend training for, and what duration would you like the training to be?
- What do you know about the training provider/facilitator?
- What will you get for the investment?

- Would you like to join a smaller or larger training group?
- What experience does the facilitator/trainer have?
- Can you transfer the information from the training directly back into your new role immediately and then in the medium term?
- Can you practice elements of the training straight away so that you don't lose the information too quickly after you have attended the training?
- Is the training primarily theoretical in its content and outcome?
- Does the training provide you with a systematic system and framework about supervision, or does it provide you with just one or two aspects of supervision?

As a guide, a one-day training can cost anywhere between $220 AUD and $550 AUD, up to a three-day training at $1,800 AUD. This gives you a guide of what type of investment may be involved and how you can use the investment wisely. There will also be times when you won't know if the investment was worthwhile until you finish the training, but for the most part, reviewing the training flyer is a great way to get a feel for the quality of the training program.

When you are looking for reputable and quality training, as a guide, Table 3.1 provides some topic areas that are important to cover in a supervision training program.

Many of these topics may also be included in intermediate and advanced training, but at a deeper and more complex level. It is also useful to have a practice component in training so that it is not just all about the theoretical perspectives of supervision.

Now that we have explored what is useful to look for in training courses on professional supervision, what do you think you might need from training to support you in your new role?

I need training to focus on the following skills for me to be a competent and skilled supervisor:

_____

_____

_____

I would like to increase my knowledge about:

_____

_____

_____

Table 3.1 Training Topic Areas

√	*How to Support and Guide Supervisees to Get the Most from Their Supervision*
	Understand the process in which professional supervision takes place, that is, what is supervision and why it is important, burnout and self-care in supervision, the process of supervision, benefits and purpose of supervision, roles and responsibilities of both parties, setting the supervision agenda, developing the supervision agreement, understanding supervision policy, confidentiality and privacy, purpose of supervision and the tasks that are required in supervision, documents, storage, etc.
	Understand the important elements of being an effective supervisor
	Explore the ethical and industrial contexts in which supervision takes place
	Explore what documents are required in supervision
	The process of reflection in supervision
	How to provide useful feedback in supervision, technical communication skills, developing a feedback framework
	Understand the different types of supervision, that is, clinical, administrative, professional, non-clinical, non-professional, formal, etc.
	Setting up a framework for culturally appropriate supervision
	Dealing with and responding to challenges in supervision
	How to reinvigorate supervision when it becomes stale or ineffective
	How to evaluate supervision for it to remain effective
	Understand the skills and competencies supervisors require to effectively undertake their role
	Supervisor communication styles
	Understand different supervisor styles and approaches
	Communication techniques and skills
	Develop a positive supervisory relationship
	How the annual review process links to supervision discussions

I need to increase my competencies/skills in the following areas:

_____

_____

_____

I already have the following qualities and attributes as a supervisor:

_____

_____

_____

Things I need from training are:

_____

_____

_____

The topic areas I would like to see in training are:

_____

_____

_____

The type of training that works best for my learning style is:

_____

_____

_____

The ideal duration of training for me at this time is:

_____

_____

_____

I need to consider the following from what others have advised about
supervision training:

_____

_____

_____

I am not that interested in the following training:

_____

_____

_____

These are the other things I need to consider to continue my professional
development:

_____

_____

_____

Now that we have explored how important training is and focused on
what you might look for in a training workshop or program, there are
other things such as having supervision yourself, reading and researching

supervision that are just as important if you find it difficult to get to training prior to commencing in your role.

Chapter 3 Summary

In this chapter, we have explored the importance of attending training prior to becoming a professional supervisor. Consider doing some research about potential training, and talk to other supervisors or colleagues. Contact or email your professional association if you are a member to talk to them about what training they can offer. Training will enhance your existing skills and knowledge, provide you with new information and give you increased confidence to go into the role.

Key points to consider regarding quality supervision training.

1.
2.
3.
4.
5.

Chapter 4

Setting the Context for Effective Supervision

> We need to realise that taking the time to reflect on a regular basis
> is the starting point for growth and change.

Silvia Damiano

You may feel somewhat hesitant about your new role and at the same time excited and keen to get started. Prior to commencing with supervisees, there are a number of things to consider when establishing the framework and process of supervision. The supervisory process includes understanding what documents are necessary to meet the ethical and industrial requirements. Supervision fits within an industrial process. This means that supervision documents can be subpoenaed or a supervisee can at any time request documents from their supervision file, particularly where the supervisor holds the file in a safe storage cabinet.

Before we get started on the process of supervision, think of an elite athlete you know of.

- What is their field of expertise?
- What do you know about them?
- How did they map out the key things they needed to do?
- What did they do to focus?
- What setbacks did they experience on the journey?
- What things did they put in place to achieve their goals?
- How did they make it to the top of their field?

- How have they maintained their peak performance?
- What have you observed about their mindset over time?
- What type of coach or mentor did they engage?
- What skills did the mentor or coach have?
- What support team did they have around them?

_____

_____

_____

_____

_____

If we think about an athlete who is at the top of their game, we have a general idea of what they needed to do to get there. An athlete has to learn the technical skills required in their field of expertise, have a specific knowledge base as well as understand the skills and competencies they need to ensure they maintain peak performance over time. They practice and hone their skills every day until they perfect them, and then some more. They always have a coach and mentor that stays on the journey with them. This person is there to perfect every aspect of their skill base, mindset, performance and techniques.

They change their approach as a coach and as the athlete hones their skills, they shape the journey of the athlete as they travel along with them. Without a mentor or coach, most athletes would not reach their goals, objectives or potential. The coach usually plays an important role in the athlete's success, and the relationship is built over time. Both parties usually stay together as coach and athlete for a long period of time.

Being an effective supervisor is much like being an athlete. Being a competent supervisor takes time, dedication, practice, commitment, knowledge, technical skills and training. It is a crucial role in the supervisee's professional work and helps to develop and grow the supervisee no matter how experienced the supervisee is. This also means that the supervisor needs to continue to grow and develop their skills and knowledge over time.

I can remember a few years ago when one of my supervisees was attending supervision training with a trainer from the UK. When she had completed the training, she bought a really great book on ethics and supervision. She proudly came to a supervision meeting excited about the book she had purchased. I laughed and shook my head! She knew exactly what I was thinking and laughed as well, saying to me that now I would need to read the book and perhaps I could keep a chapter ahead so we could then develop her ethics framework in supervision, and that's exactly what we did.

The important part of this story was that the supervisee needs me as the supervisor to keep up to date with the latest information in her area of work and continue to grow and develop as the professional supervisor. It was a great book and we enjoyed sharing our learnings from each chapter, and many years later we still have a good laugh about this. She has recently purchased another new book on neuroscience, and whilst I have a steady knowledge base in this area, yes, you guessed it, I am going to read the new book as we share the ongoing journey of learning together.

Think about your own experiences in supervision – both the positive and challenging experiences. The experiences and influences that we all have in supervision guide and impact the way that we provide supervision. Think about how you like to learn so you can understand how your supervisees learn best. There are various learning styles assessments available, and these are useful to give to your supervisee when you commence so that you can set up supervision in a way that supports your supervisee's learning, growth and development. Two of the most well-known learning styles assessments are from US theorist David Kolb (1984), where he developed a four-stage cycle of learning. The other well-documented learning styles assessment is that of Peter Honey and Alan Mumford (1986), also from the United States. Honey and Mumford (1986) further developed Kolb's (1984) work on learning styles (Kolb, 1984; Harrison & Healey, 2016; Honey & Mumford, 1986; Watkins & Milne, 2014).

Whilst it is important to understand how your supervisees learn, it is also useful to understand the personality and thinking styles of your supervisee, how you both communicate and what values both parties hold about supervision. Your supervisee may come to supervision because you are their line manager, or you may be an external supervisor and the supervisee is keen to engage in supervision. All of these things are important to consider when becoming a professional supervisor, because in some way it influences how you provide supervision in a professional context. Understanding the context in which supervision will take place can assist you as you prepare for meetings.

Consider the following questions and document what you might need to consider in the process of setting up supervision.

- Are you providing supervision within an organisation, a business or in your own private practice?
- What is the environment in which supervision will take place?
- What is the culture of supervision within the workplace?
- What role does supervision play? What type of supervision is being provided?

- Is supervision given value and priority within the organisational environment?
- Does the organisation have an existing supervision policy?
- Where and when will you provide professional supervision?
- Are you the line manager/supervisor and professional supervisor, or do you have just one role?
- Are you the external professional supervisor?
- What documents need to be prepared and implemented?
- How many staff will you be supervising?
- What roles do they have?
- How much experience have they had as a professional?
- What has been their experience in supervision over time?
- What are the reporting requirements for the supervisee and you as supervisor?
- Is there a supervision model the organisation uses?
- Is there an expectation of you attending training prior to commencing in the role, or can you start the role and attend training at a later date?
- How will we build the supervisory relationship?
- Has the supervisee ever attended supervision training?

If your organisation or professional association has a code of ethics or professional supervision standards, it is useful to go through these documents with your supervisees when you commence in the role (AASW, 2014; APA, 2014; NASW, 2013).

What do you believe are the key things you need to consider in establishing the supervision process?

_____

_____

_____

What are the key things to consider in setting up the environment in which supervision will take place?

_____

_____

_____

Great work!

Setting Up the First Supervision Meeting

Let's look at what needs to occur in setting up the process prior to or upon commencing supervision. This is the time to consider what relevant documents need to be developed and ready to go. Setting up the process and framework may take more than one meeting, so remember it does not need to be done all at once, but given that supervision documents can be requested by the supervisee and other parties, try to complete them in a timely manner.

The key tasks that need to be completed in setting up the supervision process in the first meeting or two are:

1. Set up a supervisee's supervision file.

   Some organisations require all staff to have a hard-copy file that includes tabulated sections in the file with the relevant supervision documents that may include the following:
   – Supervision agreement/contract
   – Minute template
   – Supervision policy or procedure
   – Copy of a supervision model
   – Supervision log/schedule
   – Learning and development plan
   – Copy of previous meeting minutes
   – Position description
   – Training record
   – Strategic plan (for senior staff/managers/executives)
   – Copy of relevant practice standards
   – Code of ethics
   – The supervisee's CV/resume
   – Previous annual review documents

   Some organisations are moving away from a hard-copy file, transferring record keeping to electronic files. Whichever system you use, it is important to understand the industrial nature of the documents that are relevant to the supervisory process and ensure they are treated within the bounds of privacy and confidentiality.

2. Develop a checklist (see Table 4.1) – a checklist provides an overview of all the documents that are included in the supervisees file, dates of when documents are completed and signed off, for example, supervisory agreement/contract, intake/assessment, etc. This may also include all the documents listed above that would be placed in the supervisee's file.

Table 4.1 File Checklist

√	Document	Comments
	Supervision agreement	
	Supervision policy/procedure	
	Minutes/minute template	
	Previous annual review	
	Supervision schedule/log	
	Position description	
	Supervision model	
	Supervisee's resume	
	Training record	
	Practice standards	

3. Monthly supervision schedule/log – this is a document that records the date each month that supervision takes place, the type of supervision you provided and both the supervisor's and supervisee's signatures. (There is a sample copy later in this book.) I provide two versions of an annual supervision schedule record, one for the supervisee to include in their supervision document portfolio/file and one for the organisation to place on file. They look slightly different and are great to refer back to if information is needed for any reports later on. A supervision document portfolio has a range of documents included that represents a whole supervision file.

4. Intake questions – in the first meeting it is important to get to know the supervisee. Using a range of questions, the intake document sets out clear expectations of the supervision process; the supervision model you will use; the relationship parameters; as well as roles and responsibilities of both parties. These questions are useful to come back to if issues arise at any time in the supervisory process or relationship or to check what expectations were discussed when you commenced the supervisory process. It is also useful to review the intake questions on an annual basis as things can change over the period of a year. Discussing the intake questions can take up to an hour. This will be explored in more detail in Chapter 6.

5. Copy of the supervision model – place a copy of the relevant super-vision model that you may be using on file. Some supervisors use a strengths-based model of supervision or a reflective model of supervision. I use the PASE (Practice/Professional, Administrative/Organisational, Support/Person, Educative/Professional Development) model of supervision. Remember to consider what model to use if you are providing supervision to staff from different cultural backgrounds. I use the CASE (Cultural/Professional, Administrative/Organisational, Person/Support, Educative/Professional Development) model titled Yarn Up Time. Don't worry too much about using a model when you are new in the role. The important thing is to set up the process properly and use other, more detailed tools such as a supervision model as you gain confidence and experience.

6. Discuss and sign the supervision agreement or contract ensuring it maps to the supervision policy that you use. Where possible, review the supervision policy with the supervisee in the first or second meet-ing to ensure they understand the detail of the document and what is expected. Also read through the agreement/contract together if you decide to have one. It is ideal if the policy and agreement includes the same language as this saves any confusion where the documents may have different intent because the language does not relate to each other. Both parties then sign the agreement/contract and place it in the super-vision folder. If you are using electronic documents, the supervisee places their name and signature with date in the document and this is then placed on file.

7. Supervision focus evaluation – this document provides an evaluation of the supervisory discussion at the end of each meeting and captures where the discussion has been focused. It is also important to have an evaluation tool that is also used on an annual basis to assess the effec-tiveness of the supervision itself. Your evaluation tool may simply ask the supervisee how effective the meeting was, ask them to evaluate supervision – 0 (*not effective*) to 10 (*highly effective*) – or have your own questions to ask the supervisee at the end of each meeting. It is impor-tant for both parties to define what 'effective' means so that you have a clear definition of what you are evaluating.

You can also use a scaling process to ask them different questions. You can evaluate supervision at the end of the meeting by asking the supervisee what was important in the discussion for them, what the key messages were, or what they are going to take from supervision back into their role. It is often not useful to ask the supervisee ambiguous questions such as what worked well, what did not work that well or what could have been different in the discussion. There is a power imbalance in both roles, so you want to ensure you have questions where the supervisee can provide open and honest responses. Often when I observe supervision and the supervisor asks the supervisee how they felt about supervision and what worked well or what did not, the supervisee provides feedback that the discussion was really good and they got a lot out of the supervision meeting. When I then meet with the supervisor and supervisee separately, you can get different feedback.

8. Review the supervisee's previous annual review/appraisal document where the supervisee has one. Ensure that any areas of focus for the supervisee from their annual review throughout the year is then included on the supervision agenda to explore when appropriate. You can then see what you have focused on in supervision throughout the year, and this can be included in the annual review discussion around the great work and successes the supervisee has had throughout the year.

9. Copy of the supervisee's CV/resume – I usually ask for a copy of the supervisee's resume as this can assist me to see what further training or qualifications may be needed over time. I usually review the resume with the supervisee on an annual basis and have a discussion in supervision about career planning. It also assists the supervisee to have a discussion in supervision about updating their resume on a regular basis.

10. Copy of the organisation's supervision policy or practice guidelines – this is important to have on file as it guides what the supervision process is all about. Taking the supervisee through the policy and/or practice guideline means that both parties understand the parameters of the supervision process and how things will work.

11. If you are an external supervisor, have a copy on file of any relevant contract/agreement that you may have with the organisation or business.

12. Copy of the supervisee's position description – this is useful as it keeps both parties on track when discussion is focused on line management topics. It also shows both parties what the supervisee is required to do in the role and how they will continue to meet the organisation's requirements.

13. If your supervisee is a manager, leader, etc., place a copy of the organisational or business strategic plan on file. This will assist you to maintain a focus on what the organisation requires and the supervisee can shape agenda items around the strategic or business plan for meetings.

14. Previous annual review/appraisal documents (if relevant) – having the previous annual review document in the supervision file is useful because you will be able to see what the outcome of the supervisee's performance in the role was. This will be easy if you are the line manager as it is highly probable that you have led that meeting. If you are an external supervisor, the annual review document is important as it gives you information about what might be useful to include on the agenda throughout the year.

15. Copy of the supervision model you are using to guide the supervisory discussion.

This may appear to be a lot of documentation to think about. However, if you set up a thorough process in the beginning, this provides the supervisee with a clear understanding of your commitment to supervision and demonstrates that it is a professional activity, not just a conversation that you have on a regular basis. If you run out of time in the first meeting to set up the file, which sometimes happens, the most important thing is to complete the intake questions at the least. The intake questions provide an important framework for you to get to know your supervisee and set the expectations of the supervisory process. You can then complete the other documents in the second or subsequent meetings.

You may prefer to ensure that the supervisee brings their agenda items to the first meeting, particularly if there is something they need to discuss within the supervisory environment. If you then have time, you could start to complete the intake questions and set up the file. Whichever way you decide to conduct the first meeting, remember to set up the process properly in the first couple of meetings, and then you can be satisfied it has been established well. Getting to know each other in the first meeting is more crucial than administrative documents as it sets the tone for the relationship in the longer term. Try and find a balance in setting up supervision well over the first few meetings.

These self-check questions are useful to consider as you set up the process of supervision.

Other things to consider:

- Have paper, pen and water in the supervision meeting room.
- Have a copy of the supervision policy to review in the first meeting.
- Remember to have a copy of the supervision agenda/minute template document.
- Take in the supervision model to go through with the supervisee.
- Include a copy of the supervision agreement for review.
- Set the agenda prior to the meeting or at the beginning of the meeting.
- Be present and mindful in the process so the supervisee knows you are present.
- Bring the supervision file, that is, a folder, manila folder or whatever type of file you are required to use.
- Prepare the room to reduce or minimise noise – put voicemail on your phone or turn off any mobiles.

New Supervisors Information Sheet

The following information sheet can assist you as you get to know the supervision process.

Step 1 – Preparation
  Physical checklist
- Check the physical environment, water, paper and pen, temperature, distractions, sound proof, free of distractions or interruptions, etc. Ensure you have a watch or clock on hand to check the time.
- First supervision meeting, copy of relevant documents (agreement, policy, supervision folder, position description, last annual appraisal doc, supervision document portfolio, model, etc.)
- Set up the professional supervision file
- Check the time you have any meetings or appointments after supervision to ensure adequate time (first supervision usually ninety minutes)
- Discussion on expectations, roles, etc. in line with questions in the intake and assessment document
- Discuss the format and process of what the first and subsequent meeting are all about
- Outline the supervision model that is going to be used

Your self-checklist
  - Am I clear on my framework, process and intake assessment questions?
  - My role and the role of the supervisee
  - Reporting and documenting requirements
  - Expectations of both parties
  - Appropriate supervisor style

Step 2 – Introduction

First supervision meeting:
  - Ensure the supervisee feels welcomed
  - Discussion occurs to set up the supervisory discussion and environment
  - Introduce supervision and what it is, the purpose, format, roles and responsibilities
  - Encourage the supervisee to ask you about your professional experience, if you have attended training, what supervisory experiences you have
  - Frequency of supervision sessions, meeting structure, expectations
  - Your availability and non-availability between supervision meetings
  - Review process/evaluation of supervision to ensure it is effective and produces outcomes desired
  - Reporting processes
  - Storage of supervision minutes
  - Actions and follow-up process between meetings

Step 3 – Intake process

Complete intake supervision questions, for example:
  - Has the staff member engaged in supervision before?
  - What have their experiences of supervision been like?
  - What have been the expectations of the supervisor/supervisee?
  - What do they see as their role and your role in supervision?
  - What does the staff member like from supervision within a given timeframe?
  - What would the staff member like from you as the supervisor?
  - How does supervision form part of the annual review process?
  - What is the supervisee's definition of supervision, what is their purpose for engaging in supervision and what do they see as the benefits of supervision?
  - What tasks need to be completed in the first meeting supervision?

- Are there any cultural needs that the supervisee has?
- How does the supervisee like to receive feedback?
- What is their preferred learning style?

Step 4 – Supervision agreement

- First meeting – complete the supervision agreement, both signing with a copy placed on file
- Read through the agreement to ensure the supervisee has an adequate understanding of the intent of the agreement
- Review and understand the expectations from the supervision policy – if you are an external supervisor, ensure you have opportunity to read and review the organisation's supervision policy to know what your role is and how you may need to meet the expectations of the organisation

Step 5 – Agenda

- Develop the supervision agenda together either prior to or at the beginning of each meeting. Lead off with the question, What would you like to focus on today?
- If it is not a first supervision agenda, ensure the supervisee brings agenda items to the meeting.

Step 6 – The supervisory discussion

- Check the time you both have (sixty minutes goes by quickly)
- Guide the discussion by the agenda and model if you have one
- Encourage self-awareness and reflection
- The meeting needs to have purpose and focus
- The discussion may focus on:
  - ethical issues and dilemmas
  - client/patient case discussion
  - policies and procedures
  - professional boundaries
  - skills and professional development
  - training needs
  - supporting the supervisee in their role
  - workload management
  - workplace dynamics, team functioning
  - performance appraisal processes
  - workplace issues, team dynamics
  - work flow/planning
  - setting goals – it is now the (date) ____/____/____ and I have/am

When I set goals with supervisees, I usually ask them to forecast what they see as their success thinking towards the future. For example, my language for goal setting with supervisees is, 'If we have been working together for six months, think about what we will have achieved between next June and now'. When we set goals that way, the supervisee's thinking will forecast out to June first and then work backwards. If I use the language, What do you think you will achieve in supervision over the next six months? it is more difficult for the supervisee to consider what achievements they will have made.

Step 7 – Close
  - Be aware of time, finish on time
  - Begin to close the session five minutes prior to finish time
  - Summarise the key focus of the discussion
  - Do not allow any new agenda items to come out of left field near the end of the discussion
  - Discuss action items and any follow-up to be completed before next meeting
  - Ensure supervisee leaves meeting in a positive space
  - Undertake evaluation of the discussion

Supervisor Reflection Questions

▪ What are my thoughts on our focus in the discussion today?
▪ How did the supervisee see the discussion from our evaluation?
▪ Do I think the supervision session was effective and supportive? How do I know?
▪ How did the supervisee respond in the meeting to the discussion?
▪ Is there anything I need to follow up?
▪ How did the supervisee interact during the discussion?

Completing the Supervision Agreement

There has been a lot written about having the supervisee sign a supervision agreement in the first or second meeting. Equally, there are many supervisors who do not feel the need to have a supervision agreement in place as the organisation's supervision policy or procedure is detailed enough to set the framework for supervision. Whichever way you decide to go, ensure that you review the agreement with the supervisee if you have one. Going through the document together ensures there are no misunderstandings about what is contained in any of the documents or the meaning of any of the content (O'Donoghue, 2015; Watkins & Milne, 2014).

You may already have a specific layout for an agreement that you use. If not, you can develop the detail of a supervision agreement in partnership with the supervisee. The importance of having an agreement or contract is to ensure both parties are committed to the process and view the supervisory process and framework as important.

In the first meeting, both parties explore the supervision agreement/contract to gain an understanding of the following.

The Bounds of Confidentiality

- The environment in which supervision takes place
- How to manage distractions such as phones and anticipated interruptions
- The professional relationship and expectations of both parties
- What is discussed and put on the agenda for meetings
- How minutes will be documented and stored given the ethical nature in which supervision takes place
- How supervision is evaluated
- What reporting processes may be required by the organisation (particularly if you are an external supervisor)

The importance of having a written supervision agreement:

- It represents and reflects the commitment that the organisation has to supervision.
- An agreement ensures the supervisee is aware of their responsibilities and the role that supervision plays in their work.
- It ensures the supervisor is aware of the responsibility in their role.
- The agreement ensures that meeting minutes are recorded within best practice principles, and this provides a basis for review and developing the focus of all discussions.
- It provides an understanding of professionalism and how discussions will take place in supervision.

■ The document assists both parties to develop a forum for continual review.
■ It provides clarity on how supervision will be evaluated and how often.
■ An agreement clarifies how the annual appraisal process links to supervision.
■ It encourages joint responsibility.

Key areas for the supervision agreement include

■ The objectives of supervision
■ Frequency of supervision sessions
■ Supervisor availability between supervision meetings
■ Structure of meetings
■ Practicalities – where, when, how often, how long, duration, what to do if supervision cannot be held, how to reschedule the next session, what form the supervision will take, for example, who will be involved, what model will be used, what does communication look like in between sessions
■ Responsibilities of each party
■ Process for dealing with ethical dilemmas
■ Process for review, assessment and evaluation
■ How feedback will occur and how often
■ Minute taking and record-keeping methods
■ Confidentiality and privacy
■ Grievance/complaint processes for both parties
■ If supervision is voluntary or a requirement in the role
■ Any reporting requirements

Supervision Policy

Most organisations have a clear, well-documented supervision policy. During the first supervision meeting, the organisation's supervision policy is discussed and reviewed in line with the supervision agreement/contract (Table 4.2). Both documents need to relate to each other, using the same wording and phrases. It is important to review the organisation's supervision policy together to set clear expectations and ensure the supervisee understands what they are signing, so both parties maintain the integrity of the policy.

Table 4.2 Sample Supervision Agreement

Defining professional supervision

Professional supervision is defined as a professional conversation that influences and guides professionals in accordance with organisational needs. It ensures accountability in the role and through a positive supervisory relationship, provides an opportunity for the enhancement of the knowledge, skills and competencies of both the supervisee and supervisor (Carroll 2010).

Supervision is a process whereby the supervisor coordinates, enhances and evaluates the work of the supervisee on a regular basis. The aim of supervision is to provide a supportive mechanism, address educational and developmental needs, engage in professional practice discussion and ensure administrative functions are supported in the workplace. Professional supervision is a collaborative discussion with intention and clear outcomes. It facilitates a reflective discussion focusing on the professional practices of the supervisee in a supportive and positive environment (Davys 2010).

Frequency of supervision

Professional supervision between _____ (supervisee) and _____ (supervisor) will occur on a weekly/fortnightly/ monthly/bi monthly/ad hoc basis.

Each supervision meeting will occur on a day and time agreed to by both parties. At the conclusion of each supervision meeting, a new time will be made with the supervisee to ensure that frequency is maintained or as soon thereafter as practicable for both parties. Where possible twelve (12) supervision meetings will be held in a calendar year.

Content of the discussion

Supervision meetings are designed to be intentional, purposeful and meaningful. Supervisors will evaluate the effectiveness of supervision to ensure it has clear outcomes. Discussions are aimed to support reflection on a broad range of issues, practice options and other agenda items including

- Understanding the context in which supervision works
- Aspects of the supervisee's role
- Challenges, issues, concerns relating to the workplace, clients, patients, customers, etc.
- Awareness of personal and professional beliefs and values in relation to the supervisee's practice/work context
- Developing and maintaining a professional boundary framework
- Professional identity and professional development in the role
- Workload management and team functioning
- Ethics and ethical decision making
- Organisational and role requirements

(*Continued*)

Table 4.2 (Continued)   Sample Supervision Agreement

Supervision is not designed to be used as

- Personal counselling or therapy
- Performance management or disciplinary meeting

Environment

The supervisory environment is a space to reflect and take time out from the busy work environment. For supervision to be valued and deliver effective outcomes, it is important that meetings have limited interruptions or distractions. This promotes an environment where both parties can focus and be in the present moment. Both parties need to be prepared and in the right mindset to ensure supervision remains effective. Mobile phones need to be switched off or placed on silent. If mobile phones are required to remain on, this is to be discussed and negotiated with the supervisor/supervisee before the meeting commences.

Professionalism

Supervision is a professional activity and is based on professional principles. It is vital that both parties to the supervisory process conduct themselves within agreed professional principles and have positive attributes and a respectful and thoughtful manner at all times. This includes both parties being committed to openness, honesty, transparency, ethical practice, collaboration and cooperation. This ensures effective outcomes can be achieved. Supervision is based on the supervisee's strengths, areas of growth and development and is solution-focused, generating options and solutions to be taken back into the workplace and professional practice. Open and honest communication will also ensure that both parties maintain a professional and positive relationship.

Confidentiality and Privacy

All information gathered and disclosed in supervision is confidential. However, given that supervision fits within an industrial and ethical process, supervision minutes are written within applied writing principles. Within the bounds of limited confidentiality, the supervisor has a duty of care obligation, that is, if it is brought to the supervisor's attention that there is potential harm to the supervisee, client/patient/customer or property. It is important to note that supervision sits within an ethical and industrial context and any information from supervision can be subpoenaed at any time.

If a situation arises where the supervisor is required to disclose information or limit confidentiality within the discussion this will, where possible, be discussed first with the supervisee.

(Continued)

Table 4.2 (Continued)   Sample Supervision Agreement

Supervision minutes are to be completed during or after supervision meetings for the purpose of future planning, formulating future supervision agendas and to have a record of the discussion for ethical and industrial purposes. A copy of the minutes is provided for both parties, and where possible an electronic file is set up so both parties can access supervision minutes and other relevant documents. Minutes are to be stored in an appropriately secured place to ensure privacy. Only relevant information is to be documented. The process of taking supervision minutes is at the discretion of the supervisee and supervisor. Supervision minutes are to be clear and precise, relevant to the discussion and reflect the principles of confidentiality and privacy regarding the recording of information. It is important to check what the guidelines are around storage of minutes by the organisation in which you work. You may be required to hold the minutes, or they may be stored in a personnel file or other area.

We have read, understood and agree with the details of the supervision agreement.

Supervisor Name:

Signature:

Date:

Supervisee Name:

Signature:

Date:

A copy of the supervision policy is then placed in the supervisee's file for future reference.

Wherever possible, I read through the supervision policy with the supervisee in the first meeting so that they understand the content, and it supports us both to make a commitment to enact the detail of the policy. If you do not read through the policy with the supervisee in the first meeting, then it is important to read through the supervision agreement/contract and review particular parts of the policy for discussion with the supervisee.

Knowing that you follow a proper and professional process with these documents ensures that over time, others get to know how you set up the supervision process. Further, if any issues arise regarding your supervisory practice, you know you have a clear and solid framework that includes reviewing relevant documents in the first meeting, providing integrity and credibility as a professional supervisor (McAdams & Wyatt, 2010).

Setting the Agenda

The supervision agenda provides a focus for the discussion in each meeting. It guides the discussion focus and still allows adequate flexibility to depart from the agenda when necessary. As most supervision meetings go for an hour, sixty minutes flies by very quickly, so the agenda assists both parties to keep on track and use the time wisely. The supervisee can provide agenda topics prior to or as you begin the meeting.

It is ideal to know what is placed on the agenda a couple of days prior to the meeting; however, in many cases this is unrealistic given both parties' busy workloads and lack of time, so many supervisors set the agenda at the beginning of the meeting. I usually set the agenda with the supervisee using the PASE model (see Figure 4.1) as we begin the meeting by asking the question, 'What would you like to focus on today in our supervision conversation?'

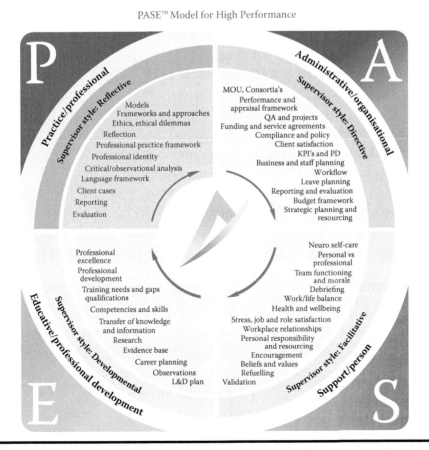

Figure 4.1　PASE model of supervision (includes words to form an agenda at each meeting).

There has been a lot written about the different functions of supervision, but there is limited information about how to engage the supervisee in supervision discussions using a well-defined and integrated supervision model. As a result, over the last ten years I have developed a suite of supervision models to support any role in an organisation, and the one to refer you to as you start your journey as a new supervisor is the PASE model of supervision.

The PASE Model

The PASE model of supervision provides a focus for the supervision discussion. Aimed at supervisees in professional and practice roles or for supervisees who are working with clients or consumers, the PASE model allows both the supervisor and supervisee to focus on different agenda items from any of the four quadrant areas. It also allows both parties to focus the discussion as soon as the meeting commences, and it assists the supervisor and supervisee to use time effectively. Given that the model has four quadrant areas in which to focus the discussion, it helps the line manager to discuss the administrative tasks and processes of the supervisee's role (Kadushin, 1993; Milne & Reiser, 2012).

The four quadrant areas of the supervision model are as follows:

PRACTICE/professional
This quadrant of the supervision model is all about working with clients. The focus of the supervision discussion includes agenda items such as professional identity, relevant interventions to use with clients, approaches used, theories, ethical decision making and how to deal with ethical dilemmas. Agenda items may also explore the language we use as a professional in the role, question types to use with clients, case/client planning, research/using the latest evidence base in the supervisee's work, and how the supervisee engages in assessment evaluation skills in their work. It is all about the practice of the supervisee as a professional in the role. When the supervision discussion focuses in this quadrant, the supervisor's style is usually reflective as there are many reflective questions that are used to explore the supervisees professional work.
ADMINISTRATIVE/organisational
This quadrant in the supervision model is all about the organisation's requirements of the role. Discussion focuses on how the supervisee adheres to their position description. Agenda items include discussion

around the tasks and processes of the role, policies and processes relevant to the role, what the organisational requirements are in the role, leave planning, workflow management, compliance, accreditation, licensing, deadlines, reporting, quality assurance, resourcing and budgets. The focus of this discussion is also about any other administrative requirements in the role. When the supervision discussion is focused in this quadrant, the supervisor's style is usually directive. This is because the line manager usually engages in the operational needs of the role and provides guidance and direction to the supervisee.

SUPPORTIVE/person

This quadrant of the supervision model focuses on the person in their role and what supports they may need to do their role well. Agenda items in this part of the supervision discussion are all about how things are going in the role, job and role satisfaction, allowing the supervisee time to debrief any personal challenges that may be impacting the workplace, supports they may require and exploration of solutions and options. The focus of this part of the supervision discussion is also about validating the supervisee, showing appreciation for their work. Validation and the discussion acts as a refuelling process. It is about minimising fatigue, stress and burnout. The supervisor uses a facilitative style of supervision when in this part of supervision as most supervisees can come up with their own answers if in a supportive discussion.

EDUCATIVE/professional development

The fourth quadrant in the model is all about the supervisee's professional development needs. Agenda items may include what training the supervisee needs, their development aspirations, career planning, integration of any learning from training or professional development back into the role, learning and development opportunities and updating training and/or review of the supervisee's qualifications. Other agenda items may include ensuring role excellence, reading, using research to inform the role, presentations at conferences for professional development and learning and development planning.

Using the supervision minute template in Table 4.3, the minutes are written up using the four quadrant areas relevant to the discussion focus. There will be times when you might start the supervision discussion in one quadrant and the focus will change, so don't worry too much about where you write the minutes. As you gain experience you will get to know where the focus of the discussion has been and write your minutes accordingly.

Table 4.3 Sample PASE Supervision Agenda/Meeting Minute Template

Name:	
Date:	
Organisation:	
Role:	

Discussion Topics:

Practice/Professional (Integrating theory to practice, framework, ethics, dilemmas, practice reflection, approaches and interventions, case discussions, case reviews, professional identity, professional excellence)

Administration/Organisational (Work flow, planning, policy, procedure, reviewing work, leave planning, organisational obligations, task and process discussion, projects, quality assurance, budgets, planning, resource allocation, accreditation)

Support/Person (Workplace morale, team development, team building, workplace identity, personal vs professional, debriefing, encouragement, validation, appreciation, job and role satisfaction, work/life balance, health and well-being, self-care planning)

Educative/Professional Development (Professional development, map to practice, review, journal articles, training needs, transfer of knowledge and information from training and conferences into the role, qualifications, competencies and skills, learning and development planning)

(Continued)

Table 4.3 (Continued)   Sample PASE Supervision Agenda/Meeting Minute Template

Actions/Follow-Up:	
Next Supervision Date:	
Signatures:	Name: _____ Signed: _____ Name: _____ Signed: _____

Supervision Schedule Record

Given the nature of supervision, it is important to document the details of when supervision takes place. Many professional associations in social work, psychology and counselling require records of meetings to be documented to show how many hours of supervision the supervisee has had over a twelve-month period. Other professionals such as human resources, legal, financial, teaching or nursing may not require such rigour to document supervision hours each year. A record of meetings can then be provided to the supervisee's professional association or kept on file in case supervision records are audited. Details on supervision are also required to demonstrate continuing professional development hours for currency of professional practice in many professions.

A supervision schedule record details the date when supervision took place, the type of supervision that was engaged, duration of the meeting and signatures of both parties. The schedule record is useful as a record that can easily identify how many supervision meetings took place through the year and when supervision was cancelled or postponed. The schedule is also helpful when reporting the use of supervision in tender and funding documents or for annual reports. When the supervisee is unwell or on annual or long service leave, this is included in the record as detailed in Table 4.4 using a code that you will document in the schedule. It is kept in the supervision file and analysed at the end of each year.

As you can see from the sample supervision schedule in Table 4.4, all meetings are recorded even if the supervisee or supervisor cancels a meeting or if the supervisee is unwell or on leave.

Table 4.4 Sample Supervision Schedule Record

Date	Supervision Type	Duration	Supervisor Signature	Supervisee Signature
5.1.2XXX	Individual	1.5hrs	Ben Thomson	Allie Hallow
5.2.2XXX	Individual	Cancelled	Ben Thomson	Allie Hallow
6.4.2XXX	Individual	1.5hrs	Ben Thomson	Allie Hallow
7.5.2XXX	Individual	1hr	Ben Thomson	Allie Hallow
8.6.2XXX	Individual/Phone	Cancelled	Ben Thomson	Allie Hallow
1.8.2XXX	Individual	1hr	Ben Thomson	Allie Hallow
2.9.2XXX	Individual	Annual Leave	Ben Thomson	Allie Hallow
10.10.2XXX	Skype	Sick	Ben Thomson	Allie Hallow
8.11.2XXX	Individual	1hr	Ben Thomson	Allie Hallow
9.12.2XXX	Individual	1.5hrs	Ben Thomson	Allie Hallow

The Supervision Structure

It is important to structure supervision meetings in a way so you do not run out of time. Allow adequate time to explore the agenda items and balance the focus areas of supervision as outlined in the PASE model quadrants already discussed, that is, professional/practice, administrative/organisational, support/person and educative/professional development. I always start supervision meetings by asking the supervisee, 'What would you like to focus on in our discussion today?' rather than, 'How are you doing, what has been happening?' This ensures we focus the discussion and use our time wisely. I usually start to wrap up the discussion with two minutes to go and then evaluate the focus of our discussion. I am always interested in how the supervisee is doing, but instead of having five minutes in the beginning of the meeting to check in, I will put that on the agenda under the S – Support/Person quadrant.

There are a number of ways to structure the supervision conversation. You may like to set an agenda with different headings, use the four quadrants of the PASE model to structure the meeting or use the four areas in Table 4.5 to focus the discussion.

However you decide to set the agenda, having a clear framework will enable the discussion to be more effective and you will be able to use the time wisely.

Table 4.5   Conversation Structure

Clients and practice	Practice/professional discussion
Supervisee focus	Support/person discussion
Organisational needs	Administrative/organisational discussion
Growth and professional development	Educational/professional development discussion

Closing the Supervision Meeting

It is important to keep an eye on the time without being too obvious or breaking the connection in the communication loop. It is also important not to conclude the supervision meeting if the supervisee is emotional or distressed. Being aware of and knowing the other person over time will assist to pick up messages and cues in relation to responses and emotions that may be present in the conversation. Keeping to the agenda and discussion will likely mean that no new agenda items will be introduced near the end of the supervision meeting.

A supervision model is a useful tool to help you finish meetings on time. The supervisee gets to know it is not appropriate to introduce a new topic in the later stages of the meeting and therefore use their discussion time wisely. It also assists both parties to know how to conclude the meeting, evaluate the discussion and carry over any relevant topics to the next meeting. This will ensure the supervision discussion ends on time with the supervisor providing a summary of what has been discussed. It also allows time to undertake an evaluation of the focus of the discussion (Watkins & Milne, 2014).

Where there is a need for more in-depth discussion that crosses into a therapeutic counselling situation, the supervisee needs referring to an employee assistance support provider (EAP). Where there is a staff conflict, or conflict between a staff member and the supervisee, it is more appropriate to refer the matter to a dispute resolution process. Do not feel as though you have to deal with this in supervision, as you are not taking the role of a counsellor or mediator in any part of the supervisory process. Whilst it is useful to know some simple mediation skills such as round up summarising or reality testing, professional mediators are well trained with specific skills and knowledge to know how to resolve any complex dispute or conflict (McBride, 2007).

End of Supervision Meeting Checklist

This is where the supervisor checks in with the supervisee about the supervision discussion to see how useful and effective it was. Asking specific evaluation questions will ensure the supervisee feels valued and provide guided reflection on what has been the most helpful in the discussion (Bishop, 2007). If you are not using a specific supervision model in which you have an evaluation process built in, the following questions at the conclusion of the discussion may assist you.

Sample Supervision Evaluation Reflective Questions

What do you see as the focus of our discussion today in each of the quadrants 0–10.
0 is *no focus*, 10 is a *high focus* of discussion in that quadrant.

_____

_____

_____

What was important for you to cover in our supervision today? Did we cover everything that you needed to?

_____

_____

_____

What key things do you feel were most valuable in our discussion today?

_____

_____

_____

Have there been any important insights for you?

_____

_____

_____

What else would you like to have discussed or thought through?

_____

_____

_____

What would you like to carry over until the next supervision session?

_____

_____

_____

What other feedback today do you have that may be useful?

_____

_____

_____

In thinking about our PASE supervision model, did we have enough of a
focus in the relevant quadrants in our discussion today?

_____

_____

_____

Supervisor Self-Reflection Checklist

At the conclusion of the supervision discussion, it is also important for the
supervisor to engage in their own brief reflective process to self-evaluate
the effectiveness of the supervision meeting. The items in Table 4.6 are
useful to reflect on and then bring forward any insights to either your own
supervision meeting or the next supervision meeting with the supervisee
(Carroll, 2007a).

Table 4.6 Supervision Reflective Evaluation

Supervisor Reflective Evaluation (SRE)
Name:
Date:
Supervisee:

Have I ensured the supervision discussion met the needs of the supervisee? How do I know that?

_____
_____
_____

What did I observe about the supervisee's engagement, discussion, responses, etc. in the meeting?

_____
_____
_____

Was there anything I need to take note of for our next meeting?

_____
_____
_____

What skills and knowledge did I bring to the meeting?

_____
_____
_____

What were my energy and focus levels like in the meeting?

_____
_____
_____

Was I well hydrated for my thinking to remain clear and focused?

_____
_____
_____

Did any of my own or the supervisee's beliefs or values influence the discussion?

_____
_____
_____

As I reflect, is there anything I could have focused on differently?

_____
_____
_____

(*Continued*)

Table 4.6 (Continued)   Supervision Reflective Evaluation

What is my evaluation of the whole meeting?
Where was the focus of the discussion in relation to the supervision model?

Chapter 4 Summary

In summary, preparing the process and getting ready for your first meeting can feel like a lot of work. However, when the process and framework are set up well, you will reap the rewards later. Developing a good relationship where rapport is built and trust developed will enable the supervisee to feel valued and supported. When you rush this process, it can give a different message. Key things to focus on in setting up the process in the first couple of meetings is the file and what is contained in it – what documents you think are important to set the scene. Try to have the policy and agreement with similar language so they refer to each other. Remember that supervision fits within an ethical and industrial process, so this part of the process is important.

Remember to

- Set the context for supervision
- Be on top of your game as a supervisor like any committed and dedicated athlete
- Reflect on what has influenced your own supervision
- Understand what reporting requirements need to be in place
- Know the culture of supervision in your organisation
- Be clear on your role
- Set up the supervisee's file with all necessary documents

Key things to consider in Chapter 4 about setting up the supervision process.

1.
2.
3.
4.
5.

Chapter 5

Conducting Subsequent
Supervision Meetings

> Well-facilitated meetings provide a space to refuel, feel heard and
> be valued as a professional.

Now that you have the supervision process and framework set up and have
completed the intake questions, supervision meetings will settle into a nor-
mal conversational rhythm. By now you will have developed rapport with
the supervisee and the supervisory relationship is well on its way to developing. Whether you provide supervision on a monthly or bimonthly basis,
subsequent meetings will follow a defined process. Whilst there is a process
now in place, it is still important to be flexible enough to meet the needs of
the supervisee and not be overly structured.

The process for subsequent meetings will now be the following:

Welcome the Supervisee to the Meeting

Develop or confirm the agenda topics for discussion.

If you have not already set the agenda, ask the question, 'What would
you like to focus on in our discussion today?' Most professional supervisors
ask the initial question such as, 'How are you today?' 'What's been happening?' or 'How are you travelling today?' This focuses the discussion within
more of a narrow emphasis. Asking the question, 'What would you like
to focus on?' provides an open space for the supervisee to set the agenda

where it is needed the most. It provides a more meaningful and purposeful start to the supervision meeting.

Focus the discussion on agenda topics included by both parties.

Ensure that supervision discussion is balanced to meet the holistic needs of the supervisee – use the PASE model quadrants to ensure that all focus areas are covered throughout the year.

Document supervision minutes as you progress through the discussion, or make dot points to write up the supervision minutes after the meeting if you need to.

■ Evaluate the focus of the discussion to ensure it has met the needs of the supervisee – you might use the reflective questions we have explored or use a scale 0–10 to gauge how effective the discussion was (0, *not effective at all*; 10, *highly effective*).
■ Both parties sign off on the supervision schedule and supervision minutes if completed in the meeting.
■ Summarise any action items.
■ Discuss any follow-up required.
■ Set another time to meet.
■ Put time in an electronic calendar, diary or schedule.
■ Close the discussion.
■ Complete supervision minutes and email to the supervisee – ensure that both parties' names/signatures are recorded.
■ Supervisor completes any follow-up actions they agreed to do prior to the next meeting (O'Donoghue, 2015).

Follow-Up in between Meetings

There will be times where the supervisee needs to touch base or consult with the supervisor on something between meetings. Internal professional supervisors may have a lot of contact with the supervisee between meetings given their proximity to each other in the workplace and the focus of the role of line manager and supervisee. If you are an internal supervisor, you will be able to negotiate in the intake meeting (first meeting) if and what type of contact you may have between meetings. As an external professional supervisor, it is also important to discuss with supervisees if and what contact can occur in between meetings via email or phone (Beddoe & Davys, 2010).

There will be times where additional supervision meetings are scheduled or where there is an urgent need for a supervision meeting that falls outside the usual schedule. No matter what contact is required, minutes need to be recorded for any discussion fifteen minutes or more and copy provided to the supervisee for their record. Some supervisees/ organisations do not require supervision minutes or a record of meetings to be documented. However, due to the ethical and industrial nature of supervision, it is advisable to complete the supervision schedule/record log and minutes or notes in case the organisation needs them in the future.

Maintaining Professional Boundaries/Feedback

There may be times as a new professional supervisor that you need to deal with reluctance, resistance and conflict situations. You may also provide supervision for supervisees who experience health and well-being or physical health challenges. You may face times where a supervisee will be experiencing issues in their personal life. It is important to know how to manage these complexities, how to provide feedback at the right time and understand the most appropriate language to use (Carroll, 2007b; Egan, 2012). Your role is not to be a counsellor or therapist, so refer to a specialist professional or agency if situations arise and the supervisee requires alternative professional assistance such as counselling.

It is equally important to remember the boundaries of the professional relationship. If you have a dual role as a line manager and professional supervisor, be mindful of how you manage any potential boundary situations. When it comes to any performance issues, there is a difference between having to deal with diminished performance in the supervisee's role and discussing the professional work of the supervisee. In most organisations, these situations are managed through a performance process. Be clear on your professional boundaries and ethical decision-making framework. If you are confronted with a difficult situation, even if you think you know what to do, feel confident to discuss this with your own supervisor so you can ensure your approach and decision are right. The most effective way to respond to challenges in supervision is through the use of particular questions and statements. Having clear communication that demonstrates care and support is crucial in the supervisory relationship.

Sustainable Supervision

Professional supervision works best if the supervisee is able to choose their own supervisor. This is often not the case when the internal line and professional supervisor are the same person. For supervision to remain effective, the following will assist in maintaining stability of the relationship:

- A committed culture of professional supervision in the workplace.
- A solid relationship built on trust, rapport and open communication.
- Awareness of the dynamics in the supervisor/supervisee relationship.
- Ensure supervision is frequent and regular.
- Rebook meetings that are cancelled or postponed, aiming for twelve professional supervision meetings each calendar year.
- Both parties engage in ongoing professional supervision.
- The supervisor has been engaged in quality professional supervision training.
- Be invested for the long term.
- Remember it is a privileged space – confidentiality and privacy are important.
- Evaluate supervision regularly through a formal framework.
- Know what and how to document supervision meeting minutes.

To provide you with an example, this scenario occurred to me a few years ago where a supervisee was engaged in an industrial hearing with their employer and the supervision minutes were requested as part of the process. The external supervisor, employee and employer had to go to the industrial tribunal. The topic of support and supervision was raised as the magistrate wanted to know how the organisation was providing support to the staff member in their role. As a result, the magistrate requested a copy of all meeting and supervision minutes as part of the hearing evidence before he handed down his decision.

If any supervision meetings are cancelled or postponed, it is useful to record on the document that supervision did not take place. This assists the supervisee and yourself as the supervisor in the future if the organisation, industrial tribunal/court or the like request details of the supervision process. It also ensures there are no gaps in information. It is much harder to look back over supervision minutes after a longer period of time and try to recall if a supervision meeting took place. Ensuring that every supervision session is documented in the supervision schedule demonstrates a history of what took place.

Supervision minutes need to only detail appropriate and relevant information. They may include what both parties may be required to do in between meetings; outline what key things you are working on in supervision; and be used to review what has been covered from previous supervision meetings (Falvey & Cohen, 2004; Hensley, 2002). It can be challenging at times to know what to record in minutes, so here are some tips for consideration. Where possible, use best practice principles in writing your minutes so they are easily followed over time.

Writing Principles for Effective Supervision Minutes

- Be precise and concise as if you were recording client notes. Supervision minutes are the same. Often meeting minutes include long and detailed information, but they do not need to be like this. Talk with the supervisee in the first meeting about what you both think is appropriate and relevant to record.
- Only write what is purposeful, meaningful and intentional. We are all busy professionals, so writing in a precise and considered manner helps to save time, ensure minutes are accurate and are easily followed.
- Map the minutes to any supervision model template you may be using. This makes the minutes easier to track in terms of follow-up and focus for the meeting.
- Ensure that any supervision minute template does not have more than four headings. Like the PASE model, any supervision agenda item fits into any of the four key headings of the model. Often supervision templates have more than seven or eight headings, and it is difficult for the supervisor to cover all headings in an hour and then document the discussion. As a guide, having a maximum of three topics for the supervision agenda can usually fit within an hour depending how much depth of conversation you go into.
- Ensure that the supervision agenda and meeting minute template(s) used are the same. Often supervisors or organisations have an agenda template, and the minute template is a different document. From a brain perspective, the supervisee has to shift focus across two documents, so try and integrate all supervision documents to have a look and feel that is the same. This will save the supervisee a lot of energy and time.

Who Is Responsible for Minute Taking?

The never-ending question is, Who takes the minutes? There are many views on this, and it is important to discuss with the supervisee who will take the minutes each meeting. I take supervision minutes electronically as I have moved away from taking any paper-based minutes; however, you will find what works best for you and your supervisees. If you take electronic minutes, it is important to ensure you cover privacy and confidentiality using passwords and security software. You may like to take a laptop into meetings, but have it to the side of you so you don't break the body language or communication. I usually document minutes as we talk and because I can type fairly fast, I get most of the relevant things from our discussion in the minutes.

I also have a supervision minute book with a copy of the PASE model on each page, so if I write the minutes in the meeting I document things so the minutes are finished in the meeting, which saves me time. Because I write the minutes using the principles of writing in the third person, they usually only take me about four minutes per supervision meeting. If you do use a laptop to document minutes during the meeting, it is crucial to maintain appropriate body language and eye contact, so you don't break the connection between you and the supervisee. When working with a new supervisee, begin without the laptop until rapport is fully built. Discuss the process of using the laptop in the intake meeting and where a supervisee prefers to have minutes recorded on hard copy, accept this request and perhaps raise it again as the relationship develops (McMahon & Simons, 2014).

Where possible, it is helpful to schedule supervision meetings a year in advance. It will save time, so you don't have to book the next meeting at the end of each meeting. I develop schedules for my supervisees each November so supervisees receive their supervision schedule in early December each year. I also follow up with sending electronic meeting requests to ensure that all supervisees have meeting times in their diaries. Even though there are times when meetings need to be changed, having supervision meetings scheduled ahead of time can assist with planning and preparation of workflow and other requirements in the supervisory role. It also assists supervisees to do their planning throughout the year as well (McMahon & Patton, 2001).

There are still times when the supervisee documents the minutes. The supervisee can change the minutes at any time to ensure they feel they reflect the conversation and they remain in the supervisee's file. Because the files are held electronically, the supervisee has access to their file at all times. It brings a sense of transparency to the process as we both share the same file, and there are always things from the file that form part of the supervision discussion agenda. If any part of the minutes need changing, or the supervisee feels there needs to be additional information, I usually ask them to change the minutes and then save in the file. We always discuss any changes first to ensure they accurately reflect the conversation. All files are password protected and the supervisee and I are the only ones to access the file.

The supervision minutes are usually written in the third person unless there are particular quotations that need to be included. Instead of saying, 'I discussed with Hannah when she is going to take her leave...', I would document, 'SV (supervision) discussion included when H is going to take her leave', or 'H discussed in supervision when she is thinking of taking leave'.

You can write your minutes using the supervisee's first name, both initials or just the first initial of the supervisee's first name. Because the supervisee's name is on the front sheet of the minutes as you see in Table 5.1, I usually only include the supervisee's first initial in the body of the minutes. This makes it quicker to record information rather than the supervisee's full name. I also refer to myself as SVor – supervisor – as this can save time when writing the minutes. Whichever way you decide to write the minutes, check if your organisation has a preferred way of documenting discussions.

Consider supervision minutes with the importance and seriousness they are meant to be regarded with. Over time, many supervisees use their minutes for all sorts of reasons. Type them up as the supervisee is going to refer to them in preparation for the next supervision meeting, or they may use information for other reporting processes in their role. I usually write brief minutes, unless there is something important to include, for example, around the supervisee's self-care or what we have focused on in relation to a client case review, etc. When the supervisee is reviewing the minutes, seeing things before them in writing can embed and anchor key messages instead of only being discussed verbally.

Where you have any concerns regarding the supervisory relationship, supervision process, the supervisee's conduct, etc., it is important to consider what to include in the minutes, and be open and transparent with the supervisee about what you are including and why. This can be difficult to maintain a positive and trusting relationship, so the use of language and

Table 5.1   Supervision Minutes (Using the PASE Model) Sample 1

Name:	Halina Simpson
Role:	Senior Practitioner
Organisation:	XXX
Date:	XXX
Topic Focus: (Mapped to the PASE Model)	P: Client review, review of SV A: S: Self-care planning E: Training program
Next Supervision:	XXX
Supervisor:	Sam Williams
PASE Focus Area	Discussion/Focus/Actions
Practice/Professional Potential agenda items: (Integrating approaches/theories/ interventions, ethics, ethical dilemmas, professional reflection, practice skills, professional knowledge base, professional identity, beliefs/values, models used, case discussions, language framework)	Case Review H provided an overview of a recent family she is working with. SV discussion focused on a review of the case and what interventions that H has been using. H indicated that she is making progress with the family and as a result the children are now attending school. SV discussion included the need for H to now focus on mum's mental health and employment opportunities given dad is beginning to engage with employment agencies. SV explored next steps in H professional approach and the need for a case review in 3 months. Review of SV SV discussion focused on influence and outcomes from SV. H indicated that she is finding that SV is assisting her to focus on client case outcomes and feeling more refreshed after most supervision meetings. H indicated she is more intentional in her work, is using the ethical decision-making framework more in her daily role and now starting to focus her team on reflecting in their work. SVor validated H in her positive engagement in SV every meeting and her willingness to complete follow-up actions and prepare for the next meeting. SVor also thanked H for her commitment to her SV and how much she has progressed in her role over the last year since commencing in the Snr Prac role.

(*Continued*)

Table 5.1 (Continued)   Supervision Minutes (Using the PASE Model) Sample 1

Actions/Follow-Up	
Administration/ Organisational Potential agenda items: (Workflow, planning, policy, procedures, leave planning, annual appraisal, position description, task and process, reporting, case notes, strategic and operational planning, monthly reporting, risk, audit, funding, tenders, agreements)	
Actions/Follow-Up	
Support/Person Potential agenda items: (Team and workplace morale, self-care, team building, personal vs professional, debriefing, avenue to be listened, encouraged, reassured, supported, giving confidence, validated, appreciated, refuelled)	SV discussion started to explore H completing her self-care plan and then working with her team to complete their plan as well. SVor encouraged H to include time twice a day to refresh given busy work load recently and increase in team numbers. The self-care plan to also include finishing work on time that allows H the space for exercise that she enjoys doing. SVor explored how self-care can also include reducing the number of meetings each week and consolidating time where the team can come together to share their successes and support each other in their roles. H stated this would assist the team as they have not had time recently to reschedule meetings for time together.
Actions/Follow-Up	H to review the current meeting schedule so the team can come together and share their successes.

(Continued)

messaging is crucial. Where you think you need to, provide more detail in the minutes and go through what you have included with the supervisee (Watkins & Milne, 2014).

To show you a couple of different examples, the first set of minutes in Table 5.1 has been written using the four quadrants from the PASE model.

Table 5.1 (Continued)   Supervision Minutes (Using the PASE Model) Sample 1

Educative/Professional Development Potential agenda items: (Professional development, how knowledge & learning is integrated from training to practice/work, review journal articles and new learning into case discussion, training needs, planning, qualifications, educational discussion)	H shared recent experience at the leadership training and how the program was useful in understanding different leadership theories. SVor enquired as to how H can transfer the learning and experience in her leadership role. H indicated that SVor would see how she will now use different language to support staff and how she will review practice cases. SVor asked H to practice during the next month and then through reflective questions to further discuss in the next supervision meeting. Discussed how learning is transferred from training back into the role and for H to notice what new experiences she has due to this.
Actions/Follow-Up	

The key focus areas are Practice, Administration, Support and Educative. Discussion topics in supervision are identified within these quadrants, and this allows the supervisor and supervisee to focus the discussion and questions from the different perspectives of the model quadrants. The second example of minutes has been included as Table 5.2 to demonstrate what to include in minutes where you have a challenging situation regarding the conduct of the supervisee in relation to continually being late for work.

The minutes in Table 5.2 have also been written using the PASE model, and you will see that they have been developed using the Support quadrant to demonstrate to the supervisee that despite being late for work a lot and it being an issue at the present time, the supervisor has raised the issue in supervision in a supportive way with the hope to having it resolved.

These examples demonstrate how the supervisor can raise the issue with Ben about the need to attend work on time, and how to document this while being supportive. If the issue continued over time, the supervisor would then talk to Ben about moving the discussion out of supervision to a performance discussion.

Table 5.2   Supervision Minutes Sample 2

Name:	Ben Hillans
Role:	Team Leader
Organisation:	XXX
Date:	XXX
Topic Focus: (Mapped to the PASE Model)	P: A: Monthly reports S: TL role E:
Next Supervision:	XXX
Supervisor:	Alina Thompson
PASE Focus Area	*Discussion/Focus/Actions*
Practice/Professional Potential agenda items: (Integrating approaches/ theories/interventions, ethics, ethical dilemmas, professional reflection, practice skills, professional knowledge base, professional identity, beliefs/ values, models used, case discussions, language framework)	
Actions/Follow-Up	
Administration/Organisational Potential agenda items: (Workflow, planning, policy, procedures, leave planning, annual appraisal, position description, task and process, reporting, case notes, strategic and operational planning, monthly reporting, risk, audit, funding, tenders, agreements)	SVor discussed with B the need for monthly reports to be completed by the 28th of each month in order for them to be reviewed. B explained the challenges in getting monthly reports completed on time over the last few months due to his busy workload. SVor explored the busy workload topic and overviewed key strategies for B to use in order to achieve the monthly reporting process. B indicated the strategies of time off line to complete the report, having quarantined time each week to keep up Team Leader (TL) reporting tasks will assist to meet the deadline of reporting each month.

(Continued)

Table 5.2 (Continued)   Supervision Minutes Sample 2

Actions/Follow-Up	Review in one month's time
Support/Person Potential agenda items: (Team and workplace morale, self-care, team building, personal vs professional, debriefing, avenue to be listened, encouraged, reassured, supported, giving confidence, validated, appreciated, refuelled)	SVor overviewed the focus for the TL (team leader). Explored the need to remain focused on getting to work on time each day, explored any circumstances that prevents B from achieving this. B indicated that there were no extenuating circumstances that influence getting to work other than having a new baby in the household. Discussed any change in work hours that the organisation may be able to support, and given that B is in a senior role the importance of achieving requirements in the role. B acknowledged that he needs to be more focused on getting to work on time and will make the commitment given his TL role. SVor thanked B for this commitment and to discuss if any further support is required.
Actions/Follow-Up	
Educative/Professional Development Potential agenda items: (Professional development, how knowledge & learning is integrated from training to practice/work, review journal articles and new learning into case discussion, training needs, planning, qualifications, educational discussion)	
Actions/Follow-Up	

Chapter 5 Summary

This chapter has reviewed how to undertake subsequent meetings and provides an overview of how to write the minutes, the type of supervision minutes you may have and two examples of supervision minutes. Taking minutes in supervision is important to keep a record of the focus of the discussion and any actions that came out of supervision. This chapter has also explored the need for appropriate professional boundaries between supervisor and supervisee. Only record information that is relevant and purposeful, be concise and precise, and adhere to privacy and confidentiality.

Key things to consider in Chapter 5 about subsequent supervision meetings.

1.
2.
3.
4.
5.

Chapter 6

Developing the Supervisory Relationship

> Building and maintaining the professional relationship begins in
> the moment when the supervisor and supervisee meet.

In the previous chapter, we discussed the context of supervision and how to set it up. In this chapter we explore how the relationship between the supervisor and supervisee develops and how to initiate the first supervision meeting. It is important to ask a series of questions in the first meeting as the relationship begins. If the supervision process commences with a clear purpose and intent as shown in Figure 6.1, it strengthens the supervisory relationship for the longer term and allows both parties to have a range of different types of conversations. Supervision has to have meaning and purpose for the supervisee for it to be an effective mechanism to perform well in the role.

Getting to Know Each Other

The first meeting is all about the supervisor and supervisee getting to know each other. It is crucial that the supervisory relationship is positive for supervision to be effective. There will be times where you have had various discussions with your supervisee prior to supervision commencing, and at other times you may have a new staff member start in their role and supervision commences almost immediately so you don't really know the supervisee all that well. As you think about how to set up the supervisory

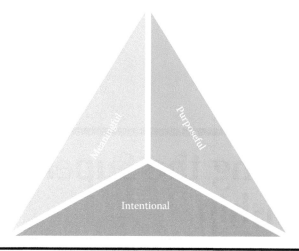

Figure 6.1   Purpose and intent of professional supervision.

relationship, consider the key things you would like to know about the supervisee and what is important for them to know about you.

What would you like to know about the supervisee?

_____

_____

_____

What is not that important for you to know about the supervisee?

_____

_____

_____

What would you like the supervisee to know about you?

_____

_____

_____

What is not that important for the supervisee to know about you?

_____

_____

_____

What Do Your Reflections from These Questions Tell You?

I know that when I consider these questions, it allows me to focus on what I need to know as a supervisor, and I better understand what is important for the supervisee to know about me.

Getting to Know the Supervisor

In the first supervision meeting, it is equally important for the supervisee to get to know particular things about you as it is for you to develop an understanding of them. These things give the supervisee an idea of who you are as a person and supervisor, what you like about your role, your passion for being a professional supervisor and an overview of your skills and knowledge (Karpenko & Gidycz, 2012).

Being aware of the initial power dynamics of the supervisor/supervisee relationship and the position of power that the supervisor initially has in the relationship, particularly if they are also the supervisee's line manager, can support the supervisee to feel more comfortable. If the supervisee knows the bounds of the relationship, how confidentiality and reporting processes will be managed, it will ensure they feel as though they can share openly and honestly in discussions from the beginning.

Consider what questions you think are useful for the supervisee to ask you that will assist to build a positive and productive relationship. Often the supervisee is unsure of what to ask about the supervisor, so it can be helpful to give them prompting questions if needed. When I ask a supervisee if there is anything they would like to know about me, my background or career and they say no thank you, I usually just give them a quick overview of some of the roles I have worked in and the types of organisations I have worked with.

Here are some areas that you might like to explore with the supervisee about yourself.

- What roles you have held
- What interests and hobbies you have
- What your own experiences of supervision have been like
- What qualifications you have
- If you are having your own professional supervision
- What your approach and process in supervision is like
- How you like to receive feedback and through what process
- How you like to communicate in professional supervision
- How you feel about being positively questioned; how you like to be positively challenged
- What feedback process you find useful in supervision
- What experience you have had in providing supervision

Let's now develop a set of questions that you think might be useful for the supervisee to ask you in the first supervision meeting.

Question 1:

_____

_____

_____

Question 2:

_____

_____

_____

Question 3.

_____

_____

_____

Question 4.

_____

_____

_____

Question 5.

_____

_____

_____

Now think about what things are not important for the supervisee to know about you.

_____

_____

_____

_____

_____

_____

Given that the supervisory relationship is an alliance where both parties need to engage in the professional environment together, it is important to remember that supervision is a two-way relationship. Taking the time to set up and develop the relationship will pay you dividends down the track. I often refer to the supervisory relationship like having points in the bank. It is important to have lots of points all of the time. Then, if you need to have any discussions that are challenging, you don't need to withdraw all the points in one conversation. Supervision is also like music; it is important to understand the tone and rhythm of the relationship, when to dance fast and when to go slow. It is all about understanding the art of attunement and how you bring all the required elements together (O'Donoghue, Wong, & Tsui, 2017).

Try not to rush the establishment process and get to know each other well. The relationship of supervisor/supervisee is one of colleagueship and understanding what your roles are and the responsibilities that come with each role. If you supervise someone who has never had the experience of supervision before, remember to socialise them into the supervisory environment more slowly by getting to know them first. After the supervisee feels comfortable with the relationship and process, I encourage the supervisee to drive the supervisory process, and because of this approach, the majority of professionals that I supervise take the process seriously and appreciate what we both bring to the relationship. Remember that each supervisee comes with different experiences and each supervision discussion is unique.

If you are unable to develop a positive supervisory alliance, it makes things much more difficult to ensure supervision provides effective outcomes. This can sometimes be the case if you are in a dual role of line manager and professional supervisor. If you find it difficult to build the relationship, it is useful to discuss this with your own supervisor and think about what strategies you could use to change the situation. Strategies to build a good relationship include having an open discussion in the intake process, understanding what the role and responsibility is of each person and being aware and conscious as a supervisor of how to develop a successful professional relationship. The supervisory role is often so busy that you can fall into the trap of being in the role without a clear focus and just going about the task and process of the role. As a supervisor you are dealing with the map of every supervisor that the supervisee has ever had (O'Donoghue, 2015).

Roles and Responsibilities

Both parties play a particular role in the supervision relationship. You will talk about this in the first or second meeting when you ask the supervisee the intake questions. As a new supervisor, it is important to consider what you think your role is. Think about the following reflective questions as a way to understand the role.

What do you think the role of a supervisor is?

_____

_____

What is the responsibility?

_____

_____

What do you think the responsibility of the supervisee is?

_____

_____

Well done. Table 6.1 includes some key responsibilities of both parties.

Table 6.1 Roles and Responsibilities

Supervisor Responsibility	Supervisee Responsibility
Ensure that supervision is set up within a defined framework	Come prepared for each meeting – have an agenda prepared prior to or at the meeting
Ensure that the required documents are completed in the first and subsequent meetings	Be on time for supervision meetings
Ensure that minutes are documented and completed for each meeting	Complete any follow-up actions in between meetings
Ensure that supervision meetings are conducted within ethical and industrial processes	Engage as an interested and active participant in supervision, take the process seriously
Build and maintain a positive and professional relationship	Participate as a positive member of the professional relationship
Both parties participate in supervision within the bounds of what is discussed in the intake questions, maintain the boundaries of confidentiality and privacy	

The Intake Process

Now that we have outlined the importance of the supervisory relationship, the next part of the process is to explore how to complete the intake questions in the first or second meeting. The intake process entails a series of relevant questions that the supervisor and supervisee discuss and document as a proactive way to establish the supervision process and framework.

The purpose of conducting an intake process in supervision is to gather relevant information from the supervisee that provides insight about their views and expectations of supervision. Intake questions assist the supervisor to make an informed assessment on what the supervisees needs, how to support them as a supervisor, and how the supervision process will work. The intake questions open up an honest and transparent dialogue that provides the supervisor with useful insight to how the supervisee thinks. They also provide a review framework for both parties if any issues or challenges occur throughout the supervisory relationship. The intake questions remain in the supervisee's file and are reviewed on an annual basis and updated accordingly. If you renew the supervision agreement on an annual basis, you may like to review and update the intake questions at the same time (Egan, 2012; O'Donoghue, 2015).

Intake Questions

The following intake questions are discussed; however, as you get to know the role or think of other questions that may be relevant, you can change what questions you discuss in the first meeting.

How would you define what supervision is? What do you think line management and professional supervision is?

_____

_____

_____

What have been your previous experiences of supervision?

_____

_____

_____

What do you see as the purpose of supervision?

_____

_____

_____

What do you see as the benefits of receiving supervision?

_____

_____

_____

How would you describe the role of the supervisor? What are your expectations of the supervisor to ensure they are effective in the role?

_____

_____

_____

What do you see as the qualities and attributes of an effective supervisor?

_____

_____

_____

To meet your supervision needs, what do you see as your learning style – how do you learn best?

_____

_____

_____

What do you see as your role in supervision?

_____

_____

_____

If you reflect towards the end of the year, what would you hope to have achieved in supervision in that time?

_____

_____

_____

What do you think is relevant or not relevant to discuss in supervision?

_____

_____

_____

Are there any specific cultural needs or social differences that you have
that you would like me to be aware of?

_____

_____

_____

Is there anything else that you think could be a barrier to supervision not
being effective? For example, health and well-being concerns, busy role,
workload, organisational challenges.

_____

_____

_____

How would you like us to evaluate the effectiveness of our supervision
discussions and outcomes?

_____

_____

_____

Are there any other questions you think that are important to ask the
supervisee in the first meeting?

_____

_____

_____

Once the intake questions are completed, either handwritten or typed,
ensure the supervisee receives a copy, restate the importance of the intake questions and that they can be reviewed at any time if any issues arise. The questions are then placed in the supervisee's file and reviewed on an annual basis.

Chapter 6 Summary

In summary, take your time to establish and build rapport. Remember to get to
know the supervisee, and ask relevant questions to show that you are interested
in what the supervisee has to say. The intake questions are useful to assist you
to get to know what the supervisee may need in supervision and will provide
you with a framework in which to come back to discussions where challenges
may present in the supervisory process, framework or relationship.

Key things to consider in Chapter 6 about developing the supervisory relationship and intake process.

1.
2.
3.
4.
5.

Chapter 7

Evaluating Supervision

> Engaging some form of evaluation on a regular basis is crucial to understand how effective supervision is over time.

Undertaking regular review and evaluation of supervision is as important as the supervision meeting itself. The question is – as a new supervisor, how do you go about evaluating the effectiveness of the supervision you are providing? How would you know that supervision is achieving what it is intended to? Most supervisors evaluate supervision by asking the supervisee how supervision is going. Whilst this is useful as it gives you a guide of how things are going as you gain confidence, it is also important to have different methods of evaluation to ensure that supervision remains effective.

Much of the research on professional supervision suggests that supervision works well if there is a collaborative relationship. Having a productive, trusting and positive supervisory relationship is crucial, but there are many other things that are also important to consider for supervision to be effective (O'Donoghue, 2015; Proctor, 2000).

There are a number of ways that you can evaluate supervision. These may include the following:

- Discussion with the supervisee on a regular basis about how they think that supervision is going. Think of the key questions you would like to ask the supervisee, and remember many supervisees will provide feedback that things are going well, but because of the power differential in the roles, the supervisee may often say that things are going well, so you may have to dig a little deeper.

- Evaluating the focus of the discussion at the end of each meeting that aligns to any supervision model that you may be using.
- Undertaking periodic formal evaluation, that is, every three to six months.
- An annual evaluation in supervision – this can also align with the supervisee's annual review process.
- Having another professional observe a supervision meeting to review the supervisory process (with consent from both parties) and provide a written report about the process and framework of supervision that shows how effective it is.

Once you feel confident in the role, get the supervisee to facilitate a supervision meeting so you can see how things are going. Then when you feel as though things are going well, with consent from the supervisee, video record a supervision meeting and critique either on your own, with the supervisee or with your supervisor. This is a great way to explore the key components of supervision and evaluate how effective supervision is.

Over time, if you video record your supervision meetings to seek feedback, it is important that the evaluation process is positive and developmental to provide you with helpful feedback that supports you to develop and enhance your technical skills, knowledge and capabilities as a supervisor. The key thing is to feel confident in any evaluation process you undertake and through your own supervision explore what things are crucial to look for.

What to Evaluate?

Next, think about what you need to evaluate. This can be quite daunting as you begin in the role as a supervisor, particularly if you are the supervisee's line manager. When you are a line manager and the supervisee is also your direct report, there are organisational and position description requirements that the supervisee has to fulfil. Usually the annual review is the place to evaluate how the supervisee is doing in their role, but not many organisations have an evaluation process that specifically looks at how effective supervision is. Given the importance of supervision, it is useful to know what impact and influence supervision is having on the supervisee and their role. It is also crucial to understand how effective you are in your role as a supervisor. It can feel a little unnerving discussing your role; however, when you undertake some form of evaluation, it provides you with great information that allows you to grow and change certain aspects of your role. The best way to develop as a supervisor is to ask the supervisee. When you develop a trusting and positive relationship, it gives the supervisee permission to be open and forthcoming with information to feed into any evaluation process (Davys et al., 2017).

There are many things you may like to consider in an evaluation framework, and the easiest way to go about this is to think about the components of the supervisory process. You could evaluate how the agenda is set each meeting, the quality of the supervision minutes, how the environment is set up with mobile phones off, little distraction, and the type of room or place where you have supervision. Other things to evaluate are your supervisory skills such as listening skills, how you reframe what the supervisee is saying, problem solving skills, how you explore ethical dilemmas, the use of language, how you provide strategies, etc.

You could evaluate how the supervisee participates in the conversation. Do they arrive for supervision discussions on time, are they prepared, do they bring their supervision folder if they have one? Does the supervisee seem committed and participate well? You could evaluate how things are followed up after the meeting, what the supervisee takes from the supervision meeting and uses in their role and what difference supervision makes in their role overall.

An evaluation framework could also be modelled around the intake questions so that the supervisee knows from the beginning what things were going to be discussed when any evaluation is undertaken.

What types of things do you think would be useful to evaluate?

_____

_____

_____

When do you think it would be good to evaluate how effective supervision is? (i.e. every three, six or twelve months)

_____

_____

_____

Now that we have explored the importance of evaluating how effective supervision is, the following evaluation will support you in your role to start thinking about what elements of supervision you are going to evaluate when you are ready. The following evaluation framework considers key elements of the supervisory framework, and you can evaluate all or some aspects of supervision every three or six months or even on an annual basis.

The first area of evaluation in this framework considers how effective the relationship has been maintained over time. It considers your communication style, the ability of both parties to manage issues as they arise and how the supervisee feels adequately supported and valued in the relationship. The second area to evaluate is the professional aspect of supervision, and the evaluation framework looks at the environment and attributes of both parties. It explores how professional identity is maintained, how confidentiality is maintained and how ethical dilemmas are explored in supervision. The third area in the evaluation is focused on knowledge and approaches in supervision. It explores how your knowledge and approach as a supervisor informs the discussion, how you use your own knowledge to contribute to the supervisee's practice and role and how you engage a supportive mentoring and coaching role.

The fourth component of the evaluation framework focuses on what supervision outcomes have been achieved. Elements to discuss include how the intake questions map to what outcomes have been achieved, if and how the supervision process links to the supervisee's annual review process and how the agenda and minutes are linked to achieving particular outcomes. The final area in the evaluation framework explores the process of supervision and includes how supervision discussions are guided by an agenda and their alignment to the supervision policy and agreement. It considers how the supervisee articulates and describes what supervision is, how both parties engage in the follow-up process and any actions that arise from supervision discussions. Each section has a comments area where you can document key parts of the discussion. Each of the sections of the evaluation is graded 5–1 and where the element is not relevant there is a code of NA = *Not Applicable*. There is no wrong or right response; the evaluation framework provides the perfect platform for an exploratory discussion with the supervisee to see how supervision is progressing (Table 7.1).

Table 7.1 Evaluation Framework

This evaluation can be undertaken on a quarterly, half year or annual basis.							

The evaluation is focused on 5–1. 5 – *Always*, 4 – *Frequently*, 3 – *Sometimes*, 2 – *Rarely*, 1 – *Never*, NA – *Not Applicable*

Supervisee Name:	Date:	Previous Evaluation Date:					
Supervisor Name:	Date:						

The supervisory relationship	**1**	**2**	**3**	**4**	**5**	**NA**
1. An effective relationship has been established.						
2. Rapport has been built and maintained.						
3. There is a clear level of comfort with each other.						
4. Both parties are aware of the supervisor's style of supervision.						
5. Supervision is flexible to meet the needs of the supervisee.						
6. The supervisor's communication style engages the supervisee.						
7. Both parties have been able to manage and resolve any issues that arise.						
8. The supervisee feels adequately supported and valued.						
9. Challenges in the relationship have been easily resolved.						

Comments:

Professionalism	**1**	**2**	**3**	**4**	**5**	**NA**
10. Clear ethics and boundaries have been established and maintained.						
11. Ethical dilemmas have been raised in supervision and explored.						
12. Both parties engage professionalism in their roles.						
13. The environment is conducive to trust and positive engagement.						
14. The supervisor positively engages and challenges the supervisee's practice.						
15. Both parties maintain their professional identity.						

(Continued)

Table 7.1 (Continued)   Evaluation Framework

This evaluation can be undertaken on a quarterly, half year or annual basis.						
The evaluation is focused on 5–1. 5 – *Always*, 4 – *Frequently*, 3 – *Sometimes*, 2 – *Rarely*, 1 – *Never*, NA – *Not Applicable*						
16. The supervisor engages insight and awareness to support the process.						
17. The bounds of confidentiality and privacy are maintained.						
18. Transparency and honestly is evident in discussions.						
Comments:						
Knowledge and Approaches	**1**	**2**	**3**	**4**	**5**	**NA**
19. The supervisor's knowledge and approaches inform the discussion.						
20. The supervisee positively contributes their knowledge in supervision.						
21. Training and development needs of the supervisee are identified and acted on.						
22. Any theories and interventions are used in supervision discussions.						
23. The supervisee engages a supportive role of coaching and mentoring.						
24. The supervision evaluation process incorporates both parties' knowledge.						
25. The supervisor engages in ongoing development.						
26. The supervisor's knowledge is relevant to the supervisee's role.						
27. There is evidence of the supervisee transferring knowledge from supervisory discussions back into the role.						
Comments:						
Supervision Outcomes	**1**	**2**	**3**	**4**	**5**	**NA**
28. The intake questions clearly map to supervision outcomes.						
29. Barriers and outcomes are identified and resolved.						

(Continued)

Table 7.1 (Continued)   Evaluation Framework

This evaluation can be undertaken on a quarterly, half year or annual basis.						
The evaluation is focused on 5–1. 5 – *Always*, 4 – *Frequently*, 3 – *Sometimes*, 2 – *Rarely*, 1 – *Never*, NA – *Not Applicable*						
30. Supervision clearly links to the supervisee's annual review process.						
31. Both parties understand and adhere to their role and responsibilities.						
32. Supervision outcomes are clearly identified and achieved.						
33. Both parties' expectations are well defined.						
34. The supervision agenda links to the supervision model used.						
35. Supervision documents are used to maintain professionalism.						
36. The supervision environment is set up in free of distractions and interruptions.						
Comments:						
Supervision process	1	2	3	4	5	NA
37. Supervision discussions are set using an agenda.						
38. Minutes are documented for each discussion.						
39. Supervision is aligned to the organisation's supervision policy.						
40. The supervision agreement aligns to the supervision policy.						
41. Both parties come well organised and prepared for supervision.						
42. The supervisee understands the process, purpose and benefits of supervision.						
43. The supervisee can clearly articulate what supervision is.						
44. Both parties engage follow-up from supervision discussions.						
45. The supervisor demonstrates a well-defined supervision process.						
Comments						

Questions to Consider

What should a supervision evaluation framework include?

_____

_____

_____

In reflecting about evaluating supervision, what things should be
considered?

_____

_____

_____

Chapter 7 Summary

Where possible, evaluate regularly. It is important to have an evaluation
framework that ensures that supervision continues to be effective and provides the desired outcomes. Evaluate the supervision discussion at the end
of each meeting and on an annual basis. This refreshes the supervision
framework and ensures the supervisee feels supported and validated. It also
provides the opportunity to reflect on your supervisory practice with the
supervisee on a regular basis. Finally, have fun in the evaluation discussion.
It is meant to be positive, useful and purposeful.

Key things to consider in Chapter 7 about evaluating supervision.

1.
2.
3.
4.
5.

Chapter 8

Capability Frameworks for New Supervisors

> Capability is a state of mind, and competency is the ability of the mind.

Whilst it is not the intent of this book to prescribe a detailed capability framework for you to follow as a new supervisor, this chapter is useful to reflect on and discuss with your own supervisor to understand the range of skills, knowledge and attributes that are important to have in your supervisory practice as you develop. As you gain experience, having a capability framework to refer to is useful as it reminds you what skills, knowledge and attributes are crucial for effective supervision.

Many supervisors feel nervous when thinking about the range of skills needed to be a supervisor, but if you have some clear indicators of what key skills and capabilities are required in your role, it provides you with a benchmark to work towards and feel confident with how you are developing in the role. It is rewarding to know that you are continuing to grow your knowledge, develop skills, hone those skills and practice them in all of the supervision meetings you undertake. Many workplaces and disciplines have a capability framework that guides supervisors in their role, and it becomes part of their continuing professional development on an annual basis (Harrison & Healy, 2016; Johnson & Stewart, 2008).

The aim of any capability framework is to

- Understand the specific set of skills, body of knowledge and attributes that a professional supervisor needs to have to support effective supervision
- Undertake a self-assessment of where you think your skills, knowledge and attributes are at any one time, so you can continue to develop as a new supervisor
- Practice the necessary skills and attributes regularly in supervision
- Measure continued growth and development in the role
- Consider what training is needed to support your ongoing development
- Be consistently aware and conscious of how you are using your skills, knowledge and attributes in supervision to support effective supervisee growth and development

Tables 8.1 through 8.3 help us review the range of skills, attributes and knowledge that supervisors need to provide effective supervision.

Table 8.1   Supervisor Skills

Planning	Reflection	Coaching	Mentoring
Analysis	Ability to hold a professional relationship	Listens accurately	Synthesises
Inspires	Forecasts	Attunes information	Uses relevant question types
Leads	Negotiates	Positively challenges with respect	Reality tests
Assesses	Evaluates	Logical	Creative
Engaging	Organised	Planned	Flexible
Collaborates	Leads	Manages	Educates

Table 8.2 Supervisor Knowledge

Ethical Frameworks	Decision Making Process	Transfer of Learning Process
Adult learning principles	Understands context	Role and layers of reflection
Range of theories and approaches	Understand the process of attuning	Human behaviour
Neuroscience	Developmental stages	Systems and organisational business systems
Methodologies	Understands process	Connections to self and others' beliefs, values and world view

Table 8.3 Supervisor Attributes

Resilient	Reflective	Emotional and Social Awareness	Integrity
Ethical	Relational	Personable	Transparent
Genuine	Authentic	Credible	Aware
Insightful	Understanding	Calm	Passionate
Vulnerable	Open	Does not judge	Encouraging

As you consider the skills, attributes and knowledge that supervisors require, choose just a few to focus on as you commence in your new role. You might like to then discuss these in your own supervision and also explore with your supervisees as it relates to their role as a professional.

These are the three skills I would like to focus on as I commence in the supervisory role.

1.
2.
3.

These are the three attributes that I would like to focus on as I commence in the supervisory role.

1.
2.
3.

These are the three knowledge areas that I would like to focus on as I commence in the supervisory role.

1.
2.
3.

Consider the key criteria below and where you would evaluate yourself as a professional supervisor currently and where you would like to be in the future. As a new supervisor, it is important to be working towards mastering the foundational capabilities that new supervisors require to provide effective supervision.

You could then develop a professional development plan with your professional supervisor to continue to evaluate your skills, knowledge and attributes in the role annually for a couple of years, then every two to three years from there. If you have an internal supervisor, it can also be useful to have an external supervisor who can mentor and support you through the early stages of your supervisory career and in time bench mark your level of capability against the following areas.

Table 8.4 sets out the capability areas and then the foundational skills and attributes that you can seek to attain as a new professional supervisor. Some of these skills and attributes may seem a little difficult to reach right now; however, as you gain confidence and experience, this framework is a great reference point to see how you progress over time. The framework does not provide a detailed or comprehensive overview of all the skills and attributes that supervisors need. It is a brief reference point to maintain insight and be conscious of what is important to consider.

Table 8.4   Sample Supervisor Capability Framework

Capability Description	Foundational Capability Details
Training	The supervisor has attended reputable training and commenced implementing information, materials, resources and tools from the training into the role. The supervisor has adequate understanding from the training curriculum about the technical skills, knowledge and competencies required to provide effective supervision. The supervisor is easily able to transfer information and learning from the training into the supervisory role.
Engagement in Supervision	The supervisor is engaged in their own professional supervision. The supervisor contributes to supervision in a positive and proactive manner, is prepared and organised for supervision meetings. The supervisee is satisfied with the quality and effectiveness of professional supervision being provided.
Supervision Process and Framework	The supervisor has a clear supervision framework in place and uses this consistently with supervisees. The supervisor has a working supervision model in place that supports the supervisory process. Supervision documents have been put in place for supervision to be effective. An effective agenda is set for each meeting. A supervision file has been set up for each supervisee with relevant documents included. The supervisor is clear about the relevant practice standards and code of ethics and has mapped these to relevant supervision documents. The supervisor engages the intake process to understand the needs of supervisees.
Knowledge of the Supervisee's Work Area	The supervisor holds knowledge of the supervisee's area of work including: • Principles and work practices • Ethical frameworks • Standards and guidelines • Relevant theories, approaches and models • Knowledge base relevant to the supervisee's work area

(Continued)

Table 8.4 (Continued)   Sample Supervisor Capability Framework

Capability Description	Foundational Capability Details
Ethical and Industrial	The supervisor understands the ethical and industrial contexts in which to provide supervision. The supervisor understands the legislative platform in which the supervisee operates. The supervisor is aware of relevant codes of conduct relevant to the supervisee's profession, the work environment and their discipline. The supervisor understands the boundaries of privacy and confidentiality. The supervisor adheres to relevant recording and reporting mechanisms. The supervisor is aware of the process in relation to informed consent and duty of care. The supervisor understands the boundaries of the professional relationship, gender, power, inequality and awareness that exists in the supervisor/supervisee relationship. The supervisor is clear on any registration requirements the supervisee may have. The supervisor has clear feedback mechanisms for resolving conflicts that may arise. The supervisor can accurately assess a supervisee's ethical conduct. Can accurately assess a supervisee's ethical conduct.
Evaluation	Has a clear evaluation framework to measure the effectiveness of supervision. The evaluation framework is integrated to the supervision model and other relevant processes. The evaluation framework is clear and concise – includes direct and/or indirect observation of the supervisory practice by another professional and has clear reporting processes.
Attributes	Engages a positive and proactive developmental approach in supervision. Can support the supervisee in a reflective manner. Is genuine, approachable, warm, focused and supportive. Honest, transparent, ethical and authentic. Builds and maintains an effective professional relationship. Can positively challenge the supervisee to support developmental growth. Has clear and open communication style. Is able to demonstrate a supportive supervisory style.

(Continued)

Table 8.4 (Continued) Sample Supervisor Capability Framework

Capability Description	Foundational Capability Details
Role/ Responsibility	Upholds relevant legislation, polices, regulations, standards and guidelines. Consults with appropriate body or other professional when ethical issues arise. Provides regular and developmental feedback to the supervisee. Provides a range of learning opportunities conducive to the supervisee's learning style and personality type. Manages conflicting situations with professionalism and support. Deals with any resistance, avoidance and reluctance effectively. Understands how to set up the supervisory process and relevant documentation.

Chapter 8 Summary

Having foundational skills and capabilities as a new supervisor takes time. If you have the opportunity to attend training, this will give you confidence and support as you commence in the role. Remember to be yourself and have the confidence to start the process. Be informed by reading articles and books on supervision, and you feel confident before you know it. You already have a set of skills and knowledge from your current and previous roles, and remember that the many transferable skills that you have gathered over time will now be present in your new supervisory role.

Key things to consider in Chapter 8 about capability frameworks and supervision.

1.
2.
3.
4.
5.

Conclusion

I hope you have gained some valuable information and tips in this book that will assist you in your journey as a new supervisor. Having the confidence to begin the journey is the first part, and having a great mentor is the second part. Gaining confidence as you grow in your supervisory role makes all the difference. This book has hopefully set you on the right path to begin. Attending training and engaging in quality supervision for yourself as well as practicing new skills will soon see you step up into the role of an experienced supervisor, no longer a new supervisor.

Providing supervision has been a career highlight for me, and I hope you enjoy your journey as much as I have. I am always keen to hear from supervisors about how they are doing in the role, understand the challenges they are faced with, and I am always available by phone or email if you have a question or two.

My email address is tracey@amovita.com.au, and I look forward to hearing from you sometime as you reflect on what you have gained from this guide and as you experience the joys of your role.

Take a deep breath and jump right in. You'll do just fine.

References

American Psychological Association. (2014). Guidelines for clinical supervision in health service psychology. Retrieved from http://www.apa.org/about/policy/guidelines-supervision.pdf.

Australian Health Practitioner Regulation Agency. (2017). Guidelines for registration standards for supervisor. Retrieved from http://www.psychologyboard.gov.au/Registration/Supervision.aspx.

Australian Association of Social Workers (AASW). (2014). Supervision standards. AASW, Canberra.

Baldwin, M. (2004). Critical reflection: Opportunities and threats to professional learning and service development in social work organisations. In N. Gould & M. Baldwin (Eds.), *Social work, critical reflection and the learning organisation*. Aldershot: Ashgate.

Beddoe, L., & Davys, A. (2010). *Best practice in professional supervision*. London: Jessica Kingsley Publications.

Bernard, J. M., & Goodyear, R. K. (1992). *Fundamentals of clinical supervision*. Needham Heights, MA: Allyn & Bacon.

Bishop, V. (2007). *Clinical supervision in practice*. Palgrave Macmillan: New York.

Blair, K., & Peake, T. (1995). Stages of supervisor development. *The Clinical Supervisor, 13*(2): 122–32.

Bogo, M., & McKnight, K. (2006). Clinical supervision in social work: A review of the research literature. *The Clinical Supervisor, 24*(1/2): 49–67.

Carroll, M. (2007a). Installing reflective supervision on your organisational hard drive. *Psychotherapy Australia, 13*(4): 26–28.

Carroll, M. (2007b). One more time: What is supervision? *Psychotherapy in Australia, 13*(3): 34–30.

Carroll, M. (2010). Levels of reflection: On learning reflection. *Psychotherapy in Australia, 16*(3): 24–31.

Davys, A., O'Connell, M., May, J., & Burns, B. (2017). Evaluation of professional supervision in Aotearoa/New Zealand: An interprofessional study. *International Journal of Mental Health Nursing, 26*(3): 249–58.

Egan, V. (2012). Australian social work supervision practice in 2007. *Australian Social Work, 65*(2): 171–84.

Egan, V., Maidment, J., & Connolly, M. (2016). Supporting quality supervision: Insights for organisational practice. *International Social Work*: 1–15.

Falendar, C. A., & Shafranske, E. P. (2007). Competence in competency-based supervision practice: Construct and application. *Professional Psychology: Research and Practice, 38*(3): 232–40.

Falender, C., & Shafranske, P. (2008). *Casebook for clinical supervision: A competency-based approach.* Washington DC. American Psychological Association.

Falender, C., & Shafranske, P. (2009). *Clinical supervision: A competency based approach* (6th ed.). Washington: APA.

Falender, C., & Shafranske, P. (2012). The importance of competency-based clinical supervision and training in the twenty first century: Why bother? *Journal of Contemporary Psychotherapy, 42,* 129–37.

Falvey, J., & Cohen, C. (2004). The buck stops here. *The Clinical Supervisor, 22*(2): 63–80.

Farmer, R. (2009). *Neuroscience and social work practice: The missing link.* Thousand Oaks, CA: SAGE Publications.

Gillet, N., Phillippe, C., Michinov, E., Pronost, A., & Fouquereau, E. (2013). Procedural justice, supervisor autonomy support, work satisfaction, organisational identification and job performance: The mediating role of need satisfaction and perceived organisational support. *Journal of Advanced Nursing, 69*(11): 2560–71.

Gonsalvez, C., Hamid, G., Savage, N., & Livni, D. (2017). The supervision evaluation and supervisory competence scale: Psychometric validation. *Australian Psychologist, 52*(2): 94–103.

Gonsalvez, C., & Milne, D. (2010). Clinical supervisor training in Australia: A review of current problems and possible solutions. *Australian Psychologist, 45*(4): 233–42.

Harrison, G., & Healy, K. (2016). Forging an identity as a newly qualified worker in the non government community services sector. *Australian Social Work, 69*(1): 80–91.

Hensley, P. (2002). The value of supervision. *The Clinical Supervisor, 21*(1): 97–109.

Honey, P., & Mumford, A. (1986). *Learning styles questionnaire.* Peter Honey Publications Ltd.

Jacobsen, C., & Tanggaard, L. (2009). Beginning therapists' experiences of what constitutes good and bad psychotherapy supervision with a special focus on individual differences. *Nordic Psychology, 61*(3): 248–58.

Johnson, E., & Stewart, D. (2008). Perceived competence in supervisory roles: A social cognitive analysis. *Training and Education in Professional Psychology, 2*(4): 229–36.

Kadushin, A. (1993). Social work supervision. *The Clinical Supervisor, 10*(2): 9–27.

Kadushin, A., & Harkness, D. (2014). *Supervision in social work* (5th ed.). New York: Columbia University Press.

Karpenko, V., & Gidycz, C. (2012). The supervisory relationship and the process of evaluation. Recommendations for supervisors. *The Clinical Supervisor, 31:* 138–58.

Kolb, D. (1984). *Experiential learning: Experience as the source of learning and development.* New Jersey: Prentice-Hall.

Kracen, A. (2015). Competency based clinical supervision: New developments in the United States. *Psycho-oncology, 24:* 35–36.

McAdams, C., & Wyatt, K. (2010). The regulation of technology-assisted distance counselling and supervision in the United States: An analysis of current extent, trends and implications. *Counsellor Education and Supervision, 49*(3): 179–92.

McBride, P. (2007). Clinical supervision and the use of structured homework. *Mental Health Practice, 10*(6): 29–30.

McMahon, M., & Patton, W. (2001) *Supervision in the helping professions: A practical approach.* Frenchs Forest NSW: Pearson Education.

McMahon, M., & Simons, R. (2014). Supervision training for professional counsellors: An exploratory study. *Counsellor Education and Supervision, 43:* 301–9.

Milne, D., & Reiser, R. (2012). Supervising cognitive-behavioural psychotherapy: Pressing needs, impressing possibilities. *Journal of Contemporary Psychotherapy, 42:*161–71.

Morrison, T., & Wonnacott, J. (2010). Supervision: Now or never: Reclaiming reflective supervision in social work. Retrieved from https://www.in-trac.co.uk.

National Association of Social Workers (NASW). (2013). Best Practice Standards in Social Work Supervision. NASW: Washington DC.

O'Donoghue, K. (2015). Issues and challenges facing social work supervision in the twenty-first century. *China Journal of Social Work, 8*(2): 136–49.

O'Donoghue, K., Wong Yuh Ju, P., & Tsui, M. S. (2017). Constructing an evidence-informed social work supervision model. *European Journal of Social Work, 1*(11): 1–11.

Proctor, B. (2000). *Group supervision: A guide to creative practice.* Thousand Oaks, CA: SAGE Publications.

Shaw, E. (2004). The 'pointy' end of clinical supervision: Ethical, legal and performance issues. *Psychotherapy in Australia, 10*(2): 64–70.

Terry, J., Gonsalvez, C., & Deane, F. (2017). Brief online training with standardised vignettes reduces inflated supervisor ratings of trainee practitioner competencies. *The Australian Psychologist, 52:* 130–39.

Tsui, M. (2005). Functions of social work supervision in Hong Kong. *International Social Work, 48*(4): 485–93.

Tsui, M., & Cheung, C. (2004). Gone with the wind: The impacts of managerialism on human services. *British Journal of Social Work, 34:* 437–42.

Wallbank, S., & Hatton, S. (2011). Reducing burnout and stress: The effectiveness of clinical supervision. *Community Practitioner, 31*(5): 31–35.

Watkins, E., & Milne, D. (Eds.). (2014). *The Wiley Blackwell international handbook of clinical supervision.* West Sussex, UK: John Wiley & Sons, Ltd.

Wolfsfeld, L., & Hay-Yahia, M. (2010). Learning and supervisory styles in the training of social workers. *The Clinical Supervisor, 29*(1): 68–94, 609–46.

Index

Page numbers followed by f and t indicate figures and tables, respectively.